THE ORIGINS OF CHRISTIAN FAITH

Terrance Callan

De La Salle House

PAULIST PRESS
New York and Mahwah, N.J.

Library of Congress Cataloging-in-Publication Data

Callan, Terrance, 1947–
    The origins of Christian faith/Terrance Callan.
        p.   cm.
    includes bibliographical references and index.
    ISBN 0-8091-3459-4
    1. Jesus Christ—History of doctrines—Early church, ca. 30-600. 2.
Christianity—Origin. I. Title.
BT198.C25   1993
232'.09'015—dc20   93-23465
                                                                          CIP

Published by Paulist Press
997 Macarthur Boulevard
Mahwah, NJ 07430

Printed and bound in the
United States of America

CONTENTS

FOR
NILS A. DAHL

ACKNOWLEDGEMENTS

I wish to thank my colleague Richard Walling who read this book in manuscript and made many helpful suggestions for its improvement.

Except where otherwise indicated, biblical quotations are from the *Revised Standard Version*. In some cases they have been slightly modified for stylistic reasons.

Abbreviations follow the suggestions of "Instructions for Contributors" found in the *Catholic Biblical Quarterly* 46 (1984) 397–408.

I.

INTRODUCTION

The faith of those who believe in Jesus today rests on many things. But its most important foundation is the faith of those who believed before them. To a great extent there are believers today because other believers have proclaimed Jesus to them—as they grew up in Christian families, as they studied in Christian schools, as they joined in the worship of the Christian church, and in many other ways. And the faith of those who proclaimed Jesus to the believers of today rests in turn on the faith of those who believed before them. And so the faith of each generation rests on that of the previous generation, all the way back to the first believers in Jesus. In a sense the ultimate origin of anyone's belief in Jesus is the faith of the first Christians.

What follows is an attempt to describe how the first Christians became believers and the development of their faith during the first decades after that faith came into being. For reasons which will be clear later (see Chapters II & III below) I regard the death and resurrection of Jesus as the point at which Christian faith came into existence. This occurred in approximately 30 CE. The development which I will describe was essentially complete by the date of the earliest surviving Christian documents, i.e., the letters of Paul. The earliest surviving letter of Paul is 1 Thessalonians, written in 50 CE. Thus I will attempt to describe the origin and development of Christian faith between the death and resurrection of Jesus and the writing of Paul's letters, i.e., during the twenty years from 30 to 50 CE.[1]

Because the earliest surviving Christian writings come from after this period, we have no direct knowledge of the origin and very early development of Christian faith. The letters of Paul make some reference to this period, and the Acts of the Apostles describes it at some length. But neither is concerned to describe theological development except with respect to whether or not Gentile Christians need to keep the Jewish law. Both sources tend to assume that the authors' own beliefs about Jesus were also those of the earlier period. Christians have always tended to make this assumption.

Since we have no direct knowledge about the origin and early development of Christian faith, we must infer knowledge of it from later Christian literature, especially the New Testament. In general I will reconstruct the development in such a way as to make the best possible sense of early Christian literature. The results will be speculative. But there is now a long history of such speculation among students of the New Testament. I will rely on the speculations of others before me, particularly those of Nils A. Dahl. It is he who supplies what I see as the crucial insights into the earliest development of faith in Jesus.

In what follows I will use early Christian literature mainly as a source of indirect information about the first twenty years of church history. However, at times I will also discuss briefly the views of New Testament authors themselves in order to illustrate some feature of the earliest period which can also be found in surviving early Christian literature.

A central question arising in any attempt to describe the origin of Christian faith is the question of the relationship between the life and teaching of Jesus and the faith of the early church. Scholarly answers to this question range from what R. E. Brown has called liberal to moderately conservative.[2] The liberal answer is that there is discontinuity between Jesus and the faith of the early church and that the latter is a distortion of the former. The moderately conservative answer is that there is continuity between Jesus and the faith of the early church, though the two are not identical. Some moderate conservatives argue that there is an implicit continuity between Jesus and the faith of the early church. This means that even though Jesus did not explicitly claim to be what the church later believed him to be, his life and teaching implied that he was what the church later believed him to be. Other moderate conservatives argue that there is an explicit continuity between Jesus and the faith of the early church, i.e., that to some extent Jesus did explicitly claim to be what the church later believed him to be.

My description of the origin of Christian faith will answer this question somewhat in the manner of moderate conservatives of the first kind. I will argue that much of the faith of the first Christians is rooted in what Jesus had said and done, and in what they had thought about him, during his lifetime. But their view of Jesus was so radically transformed by his death and resurrection that this is the real starting point for Christian faith. Explaining how Jesus' death and resurrection is the starting point for Christian faith is Dahl's crucial contribution to the reconstruction of Christian origins.

Any construal of the relationship between the life and teaching of Jesus and the faith of the early church depends on knowledge of the historical facts about Jesus. But modern New Testament scholarship is skeptical with regard to the possibility of knowing the historical facts about Jesus in any detail. New Testament scholars do not doubt that

Jesus lived, that he taught and worked miracles, and that he was crucified, but most do doubt that we can say much more than this with assurance. This skepticism is based on the view that reports of what Jesus did and said were transmitted orally for some time (thirty to forty years) before being written down. During this time, and while these things were being written down, they tended to be influenced by the faith of the people transmitting them. Thus it is difficult to distinguish with certainty between what Jesus actually did and said, and what may have come into the reports as a result of faith.

New Testament scholars have varying degrees of confidence with regard to the possibility of knowing the historical facts about Jesus. My starting point will be the gospel traditions as they stand. However, we will need to be aware that any given detail of the gospel traditions might be unhistorical.

Jesus the Christ

I suggest that Christian faith began with the belief on the part of some of his followers that Jesus was the Christ (i.e., Anointed = Messiah in Hebrew, Christ in Greek).[3] In believing that Jesus was the Christ his followers identified him with the redeemer which many Jews had long awaited from God. In Chapter II I will outline the origin of this expectation and describe it in detail. Here we can note that this expectation was widely held at the time of Jesus. One indication of this is the number of other people who were thought by some, for a time, to be the Christ: Judas son of Hezekiah (c. 4 BCE), Simon (c. 4 BCE), Athronges (c. 4–2 BCE), Menahem son of Judas the Galilean (c. 66 CE), Simon bar Giora (c. 68–70 CE) and Bar Kochba (132–35 CE).[4] It is also indicated by the references to this expectation in the New Testament. For example, according to Luke 2:26 it had been revealed to Simeon that he would not die before he had seen the Christ.[5]

'Christ' is the most common title for Jesus in the New Testament; it is applied to him in every New Testament; writing except 3 John, which makes no reference to Jesus. The title is not found in the material common to Matthew and Luke which is usually said to derive from the Q source, nor is it found in the gospel of Thomas. The reason for this may be that these are collections of sayings of Jesus; the title is infrequent in sayings of Jesus of any kind. We will discuss this further and suggest a reason for it below (see Chapter II, section 3: Jesus' Claims).

Even more significant than the widespread use of the title is the way the title is used. In the letters of Paul the title always refers to Jesus. Paul either combines the title with the name Jesus, or uses it in place of the name. As a result of this the reader of his letters can understand what Paul says about Jesus without being aware of the original meaning and connotations of 'Christ.'[6] The same usage can be found in the other writings of the New Testament.[7] This suggests that at a time before the New Testament documents were written the title 'Christ' was so closely associated with Jesus that it became virtually a second name. When the New Testament documents were written, the title was no longer the main way in which Christians explained who Jesus was, principally because most of the documents were written at least partly for Gentiles, who would not readily understand the meaning of the title. But the title was so basic to Christian faith that it was retained even as the significance of Jesus was explicated in other ways.

Another indication of the significance of the belief that Jesus is the Christ is that from early in the history of the church[8] right up to the present, the followers of Jesus have been called Christians, i.e., followers of the Christ. This suggests that what was most distinctive about them was their affirmation of Jesus as the Christ.

II.

RECOGNITION OF JESUS AS THE CHRIST: THE PROBLEM

If recognition of Jesus as the Christ was the starting point for Christian faith, we immediately confront a problem: it is not clear why Jesus was ever recognized as the Christ. Despite what most twentieth-century Christians would assume, Jesus did not closely resemble the Christ expected in the first century, nor did he clearly claim to be the Christ (as far as we can determine).

1. First Century Expectation of the Christ[1]

(a) Old Testament Background

Most twentieth-century Christians and Orthodox Jews would probably say that the Christ is promised in the Old Testament/Hebrew scriptures. This was also the view of first-century Jews. This is true, but only in a carefully defined sense. As it was understood by its original authors and readers, the Old Testament probably says nothing about the Christ as such. The expectation of the Christ arose after the writing of the Old Testament books, i.e., after about 200 BCE, by a process of reflection on, and interpretation of, the Old Testament. This later interpretation was then taken to be the plain sense of the Bible. Today we distinguish between the original meaning of the biblical text and meanings which it has acquired subsequently.

The starting point within the Old Testament for the development of the expectation of the Christ was God's promise to David that his sons would always be kings of Israel. One statement of this promise is found in 2 Sam 7:12–16. Through the prophet Nathan God promised David, "Your house and your kingdom shall be made sure for ever before me; your throne shall be established for ever."[2] This promise was literally kept from the time of David (c. 1000 BCE) until the Babylonians conquered the kingdom of Judah (c. 586 BCE). Even during that time, however, dissatisfaction with some of the descendants of David seems to have given rise to the hope for a better fulfillment of the promise.[3]

When the kingdom of Judah fell, the succession of David's descendants on the throne, and the kingdom itself, ceased. It was necessary to conclude either that God's promise was not being kept, or that it would be kept in some other way. At least some within Israel opted for the latter. They expected the future fulfillment of God's promise. Initially they may have expected the restoration of the kingdom and king within the relatively near future.[4] Eventually, however, the fulfillment of the promise to David was expected at the end of history, when God would decisively accomplish the salvation of Israel. At that point the king who would come in fulfillment of the promise was called the Christ.

The development of this expectation was part of a general transformation of Israel's expectations about the future that occurred following the Babylonian conquest. Prior to this, Israel's hopes for the future had been for blessings which were possible within the world we now inhabit—liberation from oppressors, prosperity, and so forth. But during this time many in Israel began to hope for an end to this world and its replacement by a new, perfect world. This apocalyptic expectation arose partly because of pessimism about the possibility of perfecting this world. Expectation of the Christ was often, but not always, part of this new kind of future expectation. One name for the new world to come was the kingdom of God, and the Christ would be its king.

The expected ruler of the kingdom of God was called Christ (= Anointed) because the historical kings of Israel had been anointed to signify their consecration for the task of ruling. Thus Christ was shorthand for 'anointed king.' In addition to kings, others were anointed in Israel, particularly priests. In some circles expectation of an anointed priest developed alongside, or instead of, the expectation of an anointed king. This influenced early Christian understanding of Jesus as the Christ to a limited extent, mainly as reflected in the letter to the Hebrews. But in general, when first-century Jews spoke of the Christ without further specification, they were thinking of the king who would come to fulfill God's promise to David. And when the early Christians called Jesus the Christ, they were identifying him with this figure.

(b) Expectation of the Christ

Many references to the Christ in Jewish literature of approximately the first century are simply references; extensive descriptions of the Christ are rare. The most extensive description of the Christ to be found anywhere is found in the Psalms of Solomon 17:21–39, a text probably composed in the first century BCE.

> Behold, O Lord, and raise up unto them their king, the son of David,
> At the time in which you see, O God, that he may reign over Israel, your servant,
> And gird him with strength, that he may shatter unrighteous rulers,

And that he may purge Jerusalem from nations that trample (her)
  down to destruction.
5 Wisely, righteously he shall thrust out sinners from (the) inheritance,
He shall destroy the pride of the sinner as a potter's vessel.
With a rod of iron he shall break in pieces all their substance,
He shall destroy the lawless nations with the word of his mouth;
At his rebuke nations shall flee before him,
10 And he shall reprove sinners for the thoughts of their heart.

And he shall gather together a holy people, whom he shall lead in
  righteousness,
And he shall judge the tribes of the people that has been sanctified
  by the Lord his God.
And he shall not suffer unrighteousness to lodge any more in their
  midst,
Nor shall there dwell with them any man that knows wickedness,
15 For he shall know them, that they are all sons of their God.
And he shall divide them according to their tribes upon the land.
And neither sojourner nor alien shall sojourn with them any more.
He shall judge peoples and nations in the wisdom of his
  righteousness.

And he shall have the heathen nations to serve him under his yoke;
20 And he shall glorify the Lord in a place to be seen of (?) all the earth;
And he shall purge Jerusalem, making it holy as of old;
So that nations shall come from the ends of the earth to see his glory,
Bringing as gifts her sons who had fainted,
And to see the glory of the Lord, wherewith God has glorified her,
25 And he (shall be) a righteous king, taught of God, over them,
And there shall be no unrighteousness in his days in their midst,
For all shall be holy and their king the Christ of the Lord.
For he shall not put his trust in horse and rider and bow,
Nor shall he multiply for himself gold and silver for war,
30 Nor shall he gather confidence from (?) a multitude (?) for the day of
  battle.
The Lord Himself is his king, the hope of him that is mighty through
  his hope in God.

All nations (shall be) in fear before him,
For he will smite the earth with the word of his mouth for ever.
He will bless the people of the Lord with wisdom and gladness,
35 And he himself (will be) pure from sin, so that he may rule a great
  people.
He will rebuke rulers, and remove sinners by the might of his word;

And (relying) upon his God, throughout his days he will not
   stumble;
For God will make him mighty by means of (His) holy spirit,
And wise by means of the spirit of understanding, with strength and
   righteousness.
40 And the blessing of the Lord (will be) with him: he will be strong
   and stumble not;
His hope (will be) in the Lord: who then can prevail against him?[5]

In addition to several brief references to the Christ,[6] the Dead Sea Scrolls, dating from the first century BCE and the first century CE, include the following rather extensive presentation of the Christ in a text often called the Eschatological Rule (1QSa 2.11–21):

(This is the) session of the men of renown, (selected) for the gathering for the deliberation of the community when (God) causes t(he)
Christ to be born among them. (The priest) will enter at the head of
the whole congregation of Israel and all h(is brothers, the sons) of
5 Aaron, the priests (selected) for the gathering of the men of renown.
And they will sit be(fore him, each) according to his honor. And
afterward (the Chr)ist of Israel will (sit). And the head(s of the families of Israel) will sit before him, (ea)ch according to his honor,
according to his (standing) in their camps and according to their sta-
10 tions. And all the heads of, i.e., the (fathers of, the congre)gation
with the sage(s of the holy congregation) will sit before them, each
according to his honor.

And (when they) gather (at the ta)ble of the community (or to drink
the) new wine, and the table of the community is prepared, (and the)
15 new wine (is mixed) to drink, (let no) one (extend) his hand over the
first of the bread and (the new wine) before the priest; for (he is the
one who) blesses the first of the bread and the new wi(ne. And he
will extend) his hand over the bread first, and (after)ward the Christ
of Israel (will ex)tend his hand over the bread. (And afterward) the
20 whole congregation of the community (will ble)ss, ea(ch according
to) his honor.[7]

The Dead Sea Scrolls also include the following bless-ing of the Prince of the Congregation, which may be another term for the Christ, in a text often called the Blessings (1QSb 5.20–29):

For the overseer to bless the prince of the congregation who…. And he will renew the covenant of the community with him to establish the kingdom of his people forev(er and to judge the poor with right-eousness and) to arbitrate with equi(ty for the oppre)ssed of the
5 earth and to walk before him perfect in all the ways of…and to establish (his holy cov)enant (during) the affliction of those who seek (him).

May the Lord (lift) you to an eternal height and like a tower of
    strength on a high wall
And may you (smite the peoples) with the strength of your (mouth);
    with your scepter may you destroy the earth and with the spirit
    of your lips may you kill the wick(ed,
10 With the spirit of coun)sel and eternal strength, the spirit of knowl-
    edge and fear of God. And may righteousness be the girdle (of
    your loins, and faithful)ness the girdle of your hips.
(And) may he make your horns iron and your hooves bronze. May
    you shove like a bu(ll and may you trample the peo)ples like the
    mud of the streets.
For God has established you for a scepter for rulers. (May they go)
    before (you and may they worship and may all the peo)ples serve
    you and by his holy name may he make you strong. And may
    you be like a li(on)…[8]

These three texts give some indication of the varia-tions to be found in the first-century expectation of the Christ. Specifically, the text from the Eschatological Rule speaks of the role of the Christ at the gathering of the com-munity, something that is at most intimated in the text from the Psalms of Solomon. Further, the former text emphasizes that the Christ is subordinate to the priest, something not found at all in the latter. In addition, the text from the Psalms of Solomon suggests that the Christ will purify the people of Israel,[9] but this is not part of the picture of the Christ in the Dead Sea Scrolls because the community that produced them regarded itself as the purified Israel. On the other hand, particularly if the text from the Blessings does refer to the Christ, the texts also show that there were common elements in the first-centu-ry picture of the Christ. All three texts say that the Christ is sent by God.[10] The texts from the Psalms of Solomon and the Blessings agree on additional items:

1. The Christ is personally virtuous.[11]
2. The work of the Christ is to reign over Israel,[12] i.e., to establish the kingdom of God; this is also described as being a judge.[13]
   (a) Since this occurs at a time of affliction,[14] it entails the conquest of those who afflict Israel, who are ungodly because they oppress the people of God;[15] this is the restoration of justice to Israel.[16]
   (b) It also includes dominion over the nations of the world,[17] making the kingdom of God universal.[18]

Note that at times the two use very similar language.[19] This reflects common dependence on Isaiah 11.

The picture of the Christ that we have developed is that of a political figure; he is a king. However, he is simultaneously a religious figure—sent by God to achieve religious goals. Christian discussion of the Christ has tended to distinguish between political and purely religious expectation of the Christ in order to make sense of the Christian claim that Jesus is the Christ. In the United States this tendency is strengthened by the separation of church and state. Because of this it is important to realize that the political and religious were combined, not distinguished or separated, in first-century expectation of the Christ. This was also true of the preexilic monarchy of Israel on which expectation of the Christ was based.

From the perspective of many first-century Palestinian Jews, the main thing from which Israel needed salvation was its domination by Rome. This was problematic, not only because it restricted freedom and resulted in taxation, but also because it interfered with proper acknowledgement of God. Further, many Jews looked forward to a time when the God of Israel would be recognized by the whole world. This could most easily be accomplished if Israel itself were recognized by the whole world. These goals were simultaneously religious and political. So, too, was the Christ who would accomplish them.

2. Jesus' Resemblance to the Expected Christ

As he is presented in the gospels, Jesus is both like and unlike the expected Christ. Jesus resembled the expected Christ in being sent by God and in being personally virtuous. Jesus also announced that the kingdom of God was near and called on people to prepare for it.[20] However, Jesus was unlike the expected Christ in that he did not establish the kingdom of God, at least not in any obvious literal way. Rome was not conquered; Israel did not assume dominion over the other nations of the world.

Though Jesus was both similar and dissimilar to the expected Christ, it seems that the dissimilarity was greater. Jesus did not perform the essential task of the Christ. Especially after he was crucified, it seems unlikely that anyone would have recognized him as the Christ. The words of the disciples on the road to Emmaus probably express what would have been the verdict of many about the possibility that Jesus was the Christ after his crucifixion: "we had hoped that he was the one to redeem Israel" (Luke 24:21). The form of the statement makes it clear that this is a hope which they have now (temporarily) abandoned.

3. Jesus' Claims

The gospel passages in which Jesus says, or may say, something about the Christ can be grouped into the following five categories:

(a) three times Jesus unambiguously calls himself the Christ;[21]
(b) once, others accuse Jesus of saying that he is the Christ;[22]
(c) in five passages Jesus speaks about the Christ, and it is not clear whether he is referring to himself or someone else;[23]
(d) in five passages Jesus is asked if he is the Christ, or is told that he is, and responds ambiguously;[24]
(e) in one passage Jesus may claim to be the Christ by his action.[25]

In view of the fact that the gospel writers undoubtedly believed that Jesus was the Christ, it is striking that Jesus so seldom clearly says that he is the Christ. And on closer examination there is reason to doubt that the three passages in which Jesus does clearly make this claim are historically reliable.

According to Mark 14:61–62, when Jesus was asked at his trial if he was the Christ, he replied, "I am." In the versions of this exchange found in Matthew and Luke,[26] Jesus answered ambiguously. The latter seems more likely to be historical, both because it is less likely to have been influenced by Christian faith, and because it is found in two different gospels neither of which depends on the other. Thus Mark's version of the exchange is likely to reflect the faith that Jesus was the Christ rather than the facts of history.

In John 17:3 Jesus says, "And this is eternal life, that they know you the only true God, and Jesus Christ whom you have sent." The term "Jesus Christ" is not found on Jesus' lips anywhere else, but it is very common in early Christian literature as a way of referring to Jesus. It seems likely that this passage is a place where common Christian terminology for Jesus has become part of the tradition of Jesus' words. If so, then this passage does not indicate that the historical Jesus once called himself "Jesus Christ."

In John 4:25–26 a Samaritan woman refers to the Christ, and Jesus says, "I who speak to you am he." This seems more likely to reflect Christian faith than the facts of history, both because the story is found only in the gospel of John, and because it may show the effects of early Christian reflection on the relationship between faith in Jesus and Samaritan expectations about the Christ.

Thus it seems that Jesus' ambiguous references to the Christ are more likely to be historical than are the few passages where he unambiguously says that he is the Christ. No doubt the evangelists understood the passages I am calling ambiguous as references to Jesus as the Christ. However, in themselves the passages are ambiguous. The general picture which emerges from these references is that Jesus was accused of being the Christ, spoke about the Christ and was questioned about his being the Christ. Speculation about the Christ surrounded Jesus like a cloud, but he seems to have been somewhat reserved about it.[27] That this is so will be confirmed by a closer look at some of these passages.

The most important example of a passage in which Jesus speaks about the Christ, and it is not clear whether he refers to himself or someone else, is Mark 12:35–37 and parallels. In this passage Jesus poses a problem: how can the Christ be David's son when David calls the Christ Lord in Ps 110:1? No answer is given. Jesus might have raised this question in order to reply to some problem in recognizing him as the Christ, i.e., his not being a descendant of David. On the other hand, this could simply be a discussion of what might be called a point of doctrine concerning the Christ, with no reference to Jesus intended.

Most informative are the passages in which Jesus is asked if he is the Christ, or is told that he is, and responds enigmatically. As we have already noted, in the version of Jesus' trial before the Sanhedrin found in Matthew and Luke (Matt 26:63–64/Luke 22:67–70), Jesus is asked if he is the Christ and responds ambiguously. In Matthew Jesus responds, "You have said so"; in Luke, "If I tell you, you will not believe; and if I ask you, you will not answer." Jesus neither admits nor denies that he is the Christ, he leaves the answer open. Likewise, in the accounts of Jesus' trial before Pilate (Mark 15:2–5 and parallels), Pilate asks Jesus if he is the king of the Jews, a sort of Roman equivalent of 'Christ,' and Jesus answers ambiguously. In the synoptic accounts Jesus replies, "You have said so"; in John, "You say that I am a king."

Perhaps most informative of all is Mark 8:27–33 and parallels. In this passage Jesus asks his disciples who they say that he is. Peter replies that Jesus is the Christ, and Jesus orders them not to tell anyone about him. It is not clear whether Jesus commands their silence because they are mistaken about him, or because he wishes to conceal the truth about himself. Once again Jesus' attitude toward the idea that he is the Christ is ambiguous. In Mark's version of the story Jesus goes on to speak about the suffering of the Son of man. Peter rebukes Jesus, and Jesus rebukes Peter in return saying, "Get behind me, Satan." This suggests strongly that Peter has not fully understood who Jesus is, and that this is the reason why Jesus commands silence.[28] It might also be the reason that Jesus is ambivalent about being the Christ. He does not deny that he is the

Christ, but realizes that what was expected of the Christ does not fit his own understanding of his mission very well. It does not allow for the suffering and death which Jesus foresees for himself. We see this same misunderstanding in Mark 10:35–45/Matt 20:20–28. James and John ask to sit at Jesus' right and left hand when he comes into his glory. And Jesus tells them that they have misunderstood what it means to be great among his followers. The one who wants to be first must be the slave of all, just as the Son of man "came not to be served but to serve, and to give his life as a ransom for many."

In Mark 11:1–10 and parallels Jesus enters Jerusalem and is acclaimed king. It is possible that Jesus arranged this (cf. Mark 11:2–3 and parallels), perhaps to present himself as the fulfillment of Zech 9:9—"Lo, your king comes to you; triumphant and victorious is he, humble and riding on an ass, on a colt, the foal of an ass."[29] This would be an implicit claim to be the Christ. On the other hand, it seems equally possible that the story reflects Christian faith that Jesus is the Christ rather than Jesus' own declaration in action that he was the Christ. And even if it is the latter, it is a very oblique way of claiming to be the Christ.

Summary

In surprising contrast to the faith of the early church, Jesus did not greatly resemble the expected Christ and seems to have shown great reserve toward the idea that he might be the Christ, perhaps to avoid misunderstanding. He spoke about the Christ. He might have used the title for himself occasionally. When others applied it to him, he did not clearly accept the identification, but neither did he clearly reject it. One thing that seems completely clear is that a claim to be the Christ was not central to the teaching of Jesus, as it later was central to the preaching of the early church.

III.

RECOGNITION OF JESUS AS THE CHRIST: A SOLUTION

As we have just seen, there were significant differences between what was expected of the Christ and the actual career of Jesus. Further, Jesus did not claim to be the Christ. This makes it difficult to understand why the early church said that Jesus was the Christ. This must be explained in order to understand the origins of Christian faith.

Another way to express the same problem is to ask what the connection is between the career and teaching of Jesus and what his followers later believed about him. If there were no connection, Christian faith might be rendered absurd, because Christians put their faith in an actual historical figure. What they believed about Jesus must be true of him, even if not obviously or explicitly. We have just seen that what they believed about him is not true in the sense that Jesus was exactly like the expected Christ, or that he said he was the expected Christ. So what was there about Jesus that justified his followers in claiming that he was the Christ?

1. The Death and Resurrection of Jesus

The best answer to this question is the one proposed by N. A. Dahl.[1] Dahl begins by observing that one of the

20

best established historical facts about Jesus is that he was crucified as a false Christ. According to the charge nailed to the cross, the crime for which Jesus was executed was that of being "King of the Jews,"[2] i.e., falsely claiming to be king of the Jews. According to the gospel accounts of the trial, Pilate asked Jesus if he was the king of the Jews,[3] and then referred to Jesus (mockingly) as king of the Jews.[4] Jesus was also mocked by the soldiers as false king of the Jews.[5] This is very likely to be an accurate reflection of the charge against Jesus because "king of the Jews" is not a title subsequently used by Christians for Jesus which might have come into the story of Jesus' crucifixion as it was retold in the light of faith. Nor is it a title which Jews used for the Christ, or any other king, which might have come into the story as a way of identifying Jesus with the Christ expected by Israel. When the people mocked Jesus as he hung on the cross, they did not mock him as "king of the Jews," but rather as "the Christ, the king of Israel."[6] Thus 'king of the Jews' is likely to be an equivalent of "Christ" which was comprehensible to the Romans. And its application to Jesus probably reflects the historical circumstances of his trial and execution.

We have already seen that Jesus was not identical to the expected Christ, and that he did not claim to be the Christ. But we have also seen that Jesus did resemble the expected Christ in some ways, that there was speculation about the possibility that Jesus might be the Christ, and that Jesus did not deny this possibility. Those who accused him of claiming to be the Christ, and had him executed on those grounds, must have feared that he would become the center of a popular uprising against the Romans. Since Jesus was not the true Christ sent by God to liberate Israel, this uprising would fail and Israel's oppression by Rome would become worse. This is the explanation of the accusation against Jesus given in the gospel of John. Those who resolved to eliminate Jesus said, "What are we to do? For this man performs many signs. If we let him go on thus, every one will believe in him, and the Romans will come and destroy both our holy place and our nation" (John 11:47–48). This was a realistic fear. This was precisely what happened as a result of Jewish revolts against Rome in 66 and 132 CE.

Jesus' execution on the charge of claiming to be the Christ/king of the Jews may indicate that even at his trial he did not deny the charge. Perhaps if he had, he would not have been executed. As the gospel accounts suggest,[7] even at his trial Jesus probably neither affirmed nor denied that he was the Christ. Dahl explains Jesus' silence thus, "Jesus could not deny the charge that he was the [Christ] without thereby putting in question the final, eschatological validity of his whole message and ministry."[8]

If we can be rather sure that Jesus was executed as a false Christ, it remains to be explained how this grounds the faith of his followers that he was truly the Christ. In itself it does not ground it. But Jesus' resurrection, occurring within the context of his crucifixion as false Christ, does provide the basis for this faith. In this context, Jesus' resurrection was seen as God's vindication of Jesus as truly the Christ. Coming after the human rejection of Jesus as Christ in his trial and execution, the resurrection was God's declaration that Jesus truly was the Christ.

As we have seen, there was no special connection between the Christ and resurrection; the Christ was not expected to undergo resurrection. Thus, in itself, resurrection would not imply that Jesus was the Christ. But resurrection was surely a sign of divine favor. And coming as it did after a negative judgment on Jesus by human beings, the resurrection was seen as a divine reversal of that human judgment. Since that negative human judgment was that Jesus was a false Christ, the divine reversal of that judgment in Jesus' resurrection was a declaration that Jesus was indeed the Christ. Thus the faith that Jesus is the Christ rests on the resurrection of Jesus in the context of his crucifixion as a pretender to the title of Christ. From this flow all other beliefs about Jesus, as we will see.[9]

History and Eschatology

Because of the way in which the early Christians came to believe that Jesus was the Christ, they gave the title new meaning in applying it to Jesus. Before Jesus' resurrection, and especially after his crucifixion, it seemed that Jesus could not be the Christ because he did not match what was expected of the Christ. After the resurrection the early Christians knew that Jesus was the Christ with an assurance that derived from God's action in raising Jesus from the dead. In the light of this they could see that their previous expectations about the Christ must have been wrong. If Jesus was the Christ then, rightly understood, God's promise of the Christ must have been a promise of Jesus all along, even though no one perceived that beforehand. The early Christians were like people who have been given an unexpected answer to a mathematical problem, and are then able to solve the problem because they know what the answer must be.

The single most important way the early Christians adjusted their picture of the Christ in light of their knowledge that Jesus was the Christ, was to include death and resurrection in the picture. Before Jesus was believed to be the Christ, there was no notion that the Christ would die and rise. But when the early Christians believed that Jesus was the Christ, and Jesus had died and risen, they concluded that the death and resurrection of the Christ must have been part of God's promises concerning the Christ in scripture all along. And they were able to find many scriptural predictions of the death and resurrection of Jesus, and of other details of his life, as we will see. These prophecies were found in texts not previously seen as speaking about the Christ; in light of the knowledge that Jesus was the Christ, they could be seen to be speaking about the Christ.

Thus early Christian use of the title 'Christ' for Jesus was not simply a matter of identifying him with the Christ of traditional expectation. Rather, use of the title for Jesus involved modification of the eschatological expectation of the Christ in light of the facts of Jesus' career. As a result of his resurrection after being crucified as a pretender to the title of Christ, Jesus was seen as the fulfillment of the eschatological expectation of the Christ. But because Jesus did not resemble the expected Christ, this eschatological expectation was reinterpreted in light of the facts of Jesus' career. This produced a specifically Christian understanding of 'Christ.' Such an interaction between eschatology and history is not unique to early Christianity; there are partial parallels to it elsewhere.

As we have earlier noted, in the Dead Sea Scrolls the expected Christ is subordinated to the future priestly leader of the community. While this is not unique to the Dead Sea Scrolls, neither is it part of the general expectation of the Christ. The idea that the Christ is subordinate to the priest probably reflects the priestly leadership of Israel in general in the first century, and in particular the priestly leadership of the community that produced the Dead Sea Scrolls. In other words, this idea results from connecting the eschatological expectation of the Christ with the concrete history of the people who expected him, and then adjusting the expectation to suit their circumstances.[10]

A closer parallel to early Christianity is provided by the Sabbatian movement of the 17th century.[11] In 1665 many Jews came to believe that a man named Sabbatai Zevi was the Christ. In 1666 Sabbatai Zevi was captured by the Turkish sultan and compelled to convert to Islam. His followers then concluded that because Sabbatai Zevi was the Christ, and had apostatized, it was necessary for the Christ to become an apostate, entering into evil in order to release humanity from its grip. Very much as in the case of early Christianity, the followers of Sabbatai Zevi saw him as the fulfillment of the expectation of the Christ, and then adjusted their concept of the Christ to fit the facts of Sabbatai Zevi's career. Their development of the idea of an apostate Christ is very similar to early Christianity's development of the idea of a crucified Christ.

Having believed that Jesus was the Christ because God had raised him from the dead after his crucifixion as a false Christ, the early Christians faced two distinct tasks. On the one hand it was necessary to support their belief that Jesus was the Christ by showing that he had, in fact, fulfilled the promises of God in the Hebrew scriptures. On the other hand, it was necessary to explain how Jesus was the Christ, i.e., how he did the work of the Christ, which was to save Israel and the world, since he was so different from what the Christ had been expected to be. We will examine the early Christians' accomplishment of these tasks below.

At this point however, we can observe that the early Christians were very successful, particularly in showing that Jesus was the fulfillment of scripture, but also in explaining how Jesus was the savior. They were so successful that most twentieth-century Christians are unaware that such an effort was ever necessary; they regard it as obvious that Jesus fulfilled the prophecies of the Old Testament and is the Christ. This makes it hard for such Christians to understand why some do not recognize Jesus as the Christ, particularly Jews. Realizing that it is only obvious that Jesus is the Christ if one begins by believing that this is so, allows for a much more sympathetic appreciation of those who do not see Jesus as the Christ. If one starts from the Jewish expectation of the Christ, which is the natural starting point both for Jews and Gentiles, it is not at all obvious that Jesus is the Christ. Beginning there, the most natural conclusion would be that Jesus is not the Christ. It is only if one begins by believing that God raised Jesus from the dead and thus declared him to be the Christ, that it becomes obvious that Jesus is the Christ. An awareness of the crucial role of faith in our views of Jesus is especially helpful in dialogue between Christians and Jews.

2. Jesus As the Fulfillment of Scripture

As we have noted, believing on the basis of his resurrection that Jesus was the Christ sent the early Christians to the Hebrew scriptures with the assurance that they would find there promises, previously overlooked, that Jesus fulfilled. It was particularly urgent to find promises that the Christ would die and rise, but also necessary to find other aspects of his career predicted. In what follows I will survey some of the most obvious examples of the early Christians' contention that Jesus fulfilled the scriptures.[12] More subtle correlations between Jesus and the scriptures are found everywhere in early Christian literature.[13]

(a) Death and Resurrection

The early Christian conviction that Jesus' death and resurrection were the fulfillment of scripture is expressed in general terms in 1 Cor 15:3–4, where Paul states the core of the Christian gospel thus: "that Christ died for our sins in accordance with the scriptures, that he was buried, that he was raised on the third day in accordance with the scriptures."[14] We find similar general statements in Luke-Acts. In Luke 18:31–33 Jesus says to his disciples, "everything that is written of the Son of man by the prophets will be accomplished. For he will be delivered to the Gentiles, and will be mocked and shamefully treated and spit upon; they will scourge him and kill him, and on the third day he will rise."[15] It is also possible that the first of the three passion predictions found in the synoptic gospels,[16] which speaks of the necessity of Jesus' death and resurrection, presumes that it is necessary because it is in accordance with the scriptures. John 20:9 says that before the discovery of the empty tomb Jesus' disciples "did not know the scripture, that he must rise from the dead."

In passages like these we can see the affirmation that Jesus' death and resurrection fulfill scriptural promises, but we cannot see precisely what scriptural promises they are considered to have fulfilled. And it is necessary to be specific about this because, as we have seen, the death and resurrection of the Christ was not expected before Jesus died and rose and was believed to be the Christ.

One passage that was seen as a prediction of Jesus' death and resurrection is Ps 118:22, "The stone which the builders rejected has become the head of the corner."[17] This passage could be seen as a prediction of Jesus' rejection by human beings, and his consequent crucifixion, and of his resurrection by God.[18] In 1 Peter Jesus is described as a "living stone, rejected by men but in God's sight chosen and precious" (2:4), probably referring to his crucifixion and resurrection. Several verses later Ps 118:22 is explicitly quoted (2:7).[19] The passage is also cited at the conclusion of the parable of the wicked tenants.[20] The parable does not speak of the death and resurrection of Jesus, but it does tell of the tenants' murder of the vineyard owner's son and the owner's punishment of them; this may have been understood as referring to the crucifixion and resurrection of Jesus.

Other passages were seen as a prediction of one or the other. In Rom 15:3, Ps 69:9 is seen as a prediction of Christ's not pleasing himself, probably referring to his undergoing crucifixion. In Acts 4:25–26, Ps 2:1–2 is seen as a prediction of Jesus' death. In Acts 8:32–35, Isa 53:7–8 is seen as a prediction of Jesus' death. Isaiah 53 is also seen as a prediction of Jesus' death in 1 Pet 2:22–25. In 1 Cor 1:19 Jesus' crucifixion is seen as fulfilling God's promise in Isa 29:14 to destroy the wisdom of the wise.

A number of passages that were seen as predictions of Jesus' crucifixion have influenced the telling of the story of Jesus' passion. In Mark 14:27/Matt 26:31, Jesus predicts that his disciples will fall away from him when he is arrested and quotes Zech 13:7 in support of the prediction: "I will strike the shepherd, and the sheep will be scattered." According to Luke 22:37, as Jesus and his disciples were setting out for the garden, Jesus said that Isa 53:12— "And he was reckoned with transgressors"—must be fulfilled in him. In Mark 15:34/Matt 27:46, as he hangs on the cross Jesus quotes Ps 22:1: "My God, my God, why have you forsaken me?" According to Luke 23:46 Jesus quotes Ps 31:6: "Into your hands I commit my spirit." According to John 19:36–37, Jesus' death without having his legs broken fulfilled Exod 12:46, and the piercing of his side fulfilled Zech 12:10.

In addition to these quotations of scriptural passages, the passion narrative contains allusions to scriptural passages that are seen as having been fulfilled in Jesus' crucifixion. Jesus' statement in the garden, "My soul is very sorrowful,"[21] seems to refer to Ps 42:6, "My soul is cast down within me." The statement in Mark 15:24 and parallels, that the soldiers divided Jesus' garments, casting lots for them, alludes to Ps 22:18: "they divide my garments among them, and for my raiment they cast lots." This passage is explicitly quoted in John 19:24. The statement that Jesus was offered vinegar to drink in Mark 15:36 and parallels alludes to Ps 69:21, "for my thirst they gave me vinegar to drink." In Matt 27:43 Jesus is mocked with words which come from Ps 22:9. Matthew 26:56 asserts that Jesus' arrest has occurred in order to fulfill the writings of the prophets.

Other passages were seen as predictions of Jesus' resurrection. Undoubtedly the most important was Ps 110:1: "The Lord says to my lord: 'Sit at my right hand, till I make your enemies your footstool.'"[22] This passage was understood as describing something which God said to the Christ, and enthronement at God's right hand was understood as a reference to Jesus' resurrection. There is an allusion to this passage in 1 Cor 15:25. After referring to the resurrection of Christ (vv 20, 23) Paul says that it is necessary that Christ reign until he has made his enemies his footstool. Colossians 3:1 urges readers to "seek the things that are above, where Christ is, seated at the right hand of God." Ephesians 1:20 says that God raised Christ from the dead "and made him sit at his right hand."[23] There are several similar references to the passage in the letter to the Hebrews[24] as well as one explicit quotation of the passage in 1:13. There is also a similar reference to the passage in the synoptic gospels.[25] In the course of his trial before the Sanhedrin Jesus says that the Son of man will be sitting at the right hand of God. The evangelists certainly understood this as a prediction of Jesus' resurrection in fulfillment of Ps 110:1.[26] The passage is quoted in Acts 2:34–35. After Peter has referred to Jesus as exalted at the right hand of God (v 33) he quotes Ps 110:1, implying that it speaks of Jesus. Because Jesus fulfilled this passage, Peter concludes, "Let all the house of Israel therefore know assuredly that God has made him both Lord and Christ, this Jesus whom you crucified" (v 36).

In Phil 2:10–11 Jesus' exaltation at his resurrection is seen as fulfilling Isa 45:23.

Another passage that was seen as a prediction of Jesus' resurrection was Ps 16:8–11, especially v 10—"For you will not abandon my soul to Hades, nor let your Holy One see corruption." Peter quotes this passage in Acts 2:25–28 and interprets it in v 31 as meaning that David "spoke of the resurrection of the Christ." This passage is also cited as a prediction of the resurrection in Acts 13:35.

In Acts 3:22–23, Deut 18:15–19 is seen as a prediction of Jesus' resurrection. And in Acts 13:33–34, Ps 2:7 and Isa 55:3 are seen as predictions of Jesus' resurrection.

Another passage that may have been seen as a prediction of the resurrection is Hos 6:2—"After two days he will revive us; and on the third day he will raise us up." This passage is not quoted in the New Testament but may underlie statements like that in 1 Cor 15:4 that Christ "was raised on the third day in accordance with the scriptures."[27]

(b) Jesus' Life

In addition to passages predicting Jesus' death and resurrection, the early Christians were able to find passages predicting many details of Jesus' career up to that point. In the gospel of Mark, we find a number of references to fulfillment of scripture in addition to those already mentioned. In 1:2–3 the appearance of John the Baptist is said to fulfill words spoken by Isaiah. In 4:12 Jesus' use of parables is explained as a fulfillment of Isa 6:9–10. 7:6–7 sees the Pharisees' and scribes' objection to

Jesus' disciples' eating with unwashed hands as a fulfillment of Isa 29:13. 8:18 implies that the disciples' failure to understand fulfills Jer 5:21. 11:9 implies that Jesus' entry into Jerusalem fulfills Ps 118:25–26. In 11:17 the profanation of the temple, which Jesus reverses, is seen as the fulfillment of Jer 7:11.

Matthew and Luke include most of these references to fulfillment of scripture[28] and many others besides. Matthew introduces eleven additional quotations from scripture with a special formula. The first of these passages is 1:22–23 where the virginal conception of Jesus is said to fulfill Isa 7:14. The quotation is introduced with the words: "All this took place to fulfill what the Lord had spoken by the prophet."[29] This group of quotations seems to be the result of special effort to link the career of Jesus with scriptural predictions. In addition to these passages Matthew makes other references to Jesus' career as a fulfillment of scripture. In 10:35–36 the divided reaction to Jesus is presented as fulfillment of Mic 7:6. In 11:10 John the Baptist is seen as a fulfillment of Exod 23:20 and Mal 3:1. In 11:23 the failure of Capernaum to repent is seen as a fulfillment of Isa 14:13, 15. In 21:16 the children's acclamation of Jesus is said to fulfill Ps 8:3.

Luke includes all of the latter group of passages except 21:16. In addition 1:17 presents John the Baptist as the fulfillment of Mal 4:5–6. And in 4:18–21 Jesus is said to be the fulfillment of Isa 61:1–2. More often than he cites particular passages, Luke simply says that Jesus is the fulfillment of God's promises. The prologue presents the entire gospel as a narrative of the "things fulfilled among us" [my translation] (1:1). The canticles of Mary (1:54–55) and especially of Zechariah (1:70–72) speak of the births of Jesus and John as the fulfillment of God's promises to Israel.

The gospel of John also makes reference to ways in

which the career of Jesus fulfilled scripture. In 1:23 John the Baptist is presented as the fulfillment of Isa 40:3. In 2:17 Jesus' cleansing of the temple is seen as fulfillment of Ps 69:9. In 6:45 belief in Jesus is seen as a fulfillment of Isa 54:13. 12:13 implies that Jesus' entry into Jerusalem fulfills Ps 118:25–26. In vv 14–15 his riding on a donkey is said to fulfill Zech 9:9. And in 12:37–40, the unbelief of the people is presented as fulfillment of Isa 53:1 and 6:10. In 13:18 Judas' betrayal of Jesus is seen as fulfillment of Ps 41:9. In 15:25 people's hatred of Jesus is said to fulfill Pss 35:19; 69:4. And in 5:39, 46 we find the general statement that scripture speaks of Jesus.

(c) Implications and Aftermath of Jesus

Not only did the early Christians support their belief that Jesus was the Christ by arguing that his life, death and resurrection fulfilled scripture, they also supported it by arguing that what emerged from his life, death and resurrection fulfilled scripture. We might say they argued that the church also fulfilled scripture.

One example of this is found in Acts 1:20 where the replacement of Judas among the twelve is seen as having been predicted in Pss 69:25 and 109:8.

In Acts 2:17–21 the descent of the Holy Spirit upon the followers of Jesus is interpreted as the fulfillment of Joel 2:28–32. Ephesians 4:8 sees Christ's ascension and giving of gifts as a fulfillment of Ps 68:18. These gifts may be understood as gifts of the Spirit (cf. 4:4). And 1 Cor 2:9 implies that the Spirit's revelation to followers of Jesus fulfills Isa 64:4.

In several places the efforts of Jesus' followers to bring good news to the world are seen as fulfilling scripture. In Rom 10:18 the Christian mission is seen as the fulfillment of Ps 19:4. In Rom 15:21 Paul sees his own practice of preaching the gospel where it has not previously been preached as fulfilling Isa 52:15. In 2 Cor 6:2 Paul sees the proclamation of the gospel as fulfilling Isa 48:9. In Acts 3:25 the Christian mission is seen as fulfilling Gen 22:18, and in 1 Pet 1:24–25 it is seen as a fulfillment of Isa 40:6–8.

The single item most often seen as having been predicted in scripture is the inclusion of Gentiles among the followers of Jesus. After the death and resurrection of Jesus, this is probably the most unexpected element of early Christianity and consequently the one most requiring justification. In his letter to the Romans Paul appeals to several different passages as predictions of the inclusion of Gentiles among the early Christians. In 9:25–26 he appeals to Hos 2:23 and 1:10. 1 Peter 2:10 also appeals to the first of these. In Rom 10:19–20 Paul appeals to Deut 32:21 and Isa 65:1. And in 15:9–12 he appeals to four different passages.[30] In Eph 2:17 inclusion of Gentiles is seen as fulfilling Isa 57:19. In Acts 13:47[31] the inclusion of Gentiles is seen as the fulfillment of Isa 49:6, and in Acts 15:16–17 it is seen as fulfilling Amos 9:11–12.

Another thing often seen as fulfilling scripture is the Jewish rejection of the Christian gospel. In Romans, Paul sees this as fulfilling a number of passages. In 9:27–33 he sees the unbelief of Israel as fulfilling three passages from Isaiah.[32] In 10:16 he sees it as the fulfillment of Isa 53:1. In 10:21 he sees it as fulfilling Isa 65:2. And in 11:8–10 he sees the unbelief of Israel as fulfilling Deut 29:4 and Ps 69:22–23. Acts 28:26–27 sees the unbelief of Israel as the fulfillment of Isa 6:9–10.[33]

(d) Jesus as Fulfillment of Scripture in Luke-Acts

As we have seen from the foregoing survey, explicit argument that Jesus and early Christianity fulfilled scripture is very common in the New Testament. It is most common in the gospels because they consist of an extensive narration of the life, death and resurrection of Jesus. And it is most common of all in Luke-Acts because it includes a detailed account of early church history. The gospels and Luke-Acts not only argue that Jesus was the Christ, but also go on to explain how he functioned as the Christ.[34] However, the former dominates the synoptic gospels and especially Luke-Acts. As we have already noted, Luke-Acts begins in Luke 1:1 with a reference to its entire content as the "things fulfilled among us" [my translation]. After a general reference to the birth of Jesus as the fulfillment of what God had promised to Israel in Luke 1:54–55, Luke-Acts presents Jesus as the fulfillment of Isa 61:1–2 in Luke 4:18–21, and follows that by showing many details of Jesus' career as the fulfillment of scripture.

Likewise, Luke-Acts says generally that the death and resurrection of Jesus fulfilled scripture[35] and supports this by suggesting that the death and resurrection of Jesus fulfilled Ps 118:22.[36] Luke-Acts presents the death of Jesus as fulfilling Ps 2:1–2 in Acts 4:25–26, and Isa 53:7–8 in Acts 8:32–35, and shows that many details of Jesus' suffering and death fulfilled scripture. Luke-Acts presents the resurrection of Jesus as fulfilling Ps 110:1;[37] Ps 16:8–11;[38] Deut 18:15–19;[39] Ps 2:7 and Isa 55:3.[40]

A special feature of the argument that Jesus fulfilled scripture in Luke-Acts is the use of what N. A. Dahl has called a two-step proof from prophecy.[41] In addition to simply saying that certain passages were fulfilled by Jesus, at times Luke-Acts makes such a connection in two steps: first, the promises of scripture concerning the Christ are described; and second, Luke-Acts argues that Jesus fulfilled these promises and is therefore the Christ. This is clearest in Acts 17:2–3. According to this passage, Paul argued with the Jews of Thessalonica "from the scriptures, explaining and proving that it was necessary for the Christ to suffer and rise from the dead, and saying, 'This Jesus, whom I proclaim to you, is the Christ.'"[42]

And finally Luke-Acts presents the early church as the fulfillment of scripture. Most notably the descent of the Holy Spirit on the church is presented as the fulfillment of Joel 2:28–32 in Acts 2:17–21; inclusion of Gentiles in the church without keeping the Jewish law is said to fulfill Amos 9:11–12 in Acts 15:16–17; and Israel's unbelief to fulfill Isa 6:9–10 in Acts 28:26–27.

This emphasis on the argument that Jesus fulfilled scripture and thus is the Christ, probably explains why the understanding of Jesus presented by Luke-Acts seems unsatisfactory to many interpreters.[43] Luke-Acts is most concerned with making the claim that Jesus is the Christ credible, something the early Christians urgently needed to do. But taking up this issue so thoroughly leaves little opportunity to explain how Jesus functioned as the Christ. And this makes the account of Jesus in Luke-Acts seem incomplete.

This emphasis in Luke-Acts may indicate that Luke-Acts is addressing Jewish concerns about Jesus.[44] This is true of other early Christian literature, outside the New Testament, that emphasizes the argument that Jesus fulfills the Hebrew scriptures.[45]

OLD TESTAMENT PASSAGES FULFILLED BY JESUS THE CHRIST

Jesus' Death and Resurrection	Jesus' Death	Jesus' Resurrection	Details of Jesus' Life
Ps 118:22	Isa 29:14 53:7–8, 12 Zech 12:10 13:7 Ps 2:1–2 22:1, 9, 18 31:6 42:6 69:9, 21	Deut 18:15–18 Isa 45:23 55:3 Hos 6:2 Ps 2:7 8:6 16:8–11 110:1	Exod 23:20 Isa 6:9–10 7:14 14:13, 15 29:13 40:3 53:1 54:13 61:1–2 Jer 5:21 7:11 Mic 7:6 Zech 9:9 Mal 3:1 4:5–6 Ps 8:3 35:13 41:9 69:4, 9 118:25–26

Descent of Holy Spirit on Church	Mission of Church	Inclusion of Gentiles	Unbelief of Israel
Isa 64:4 Joel 2:28–32 Ps 68:18	Gen 22:18 Isa 40:6–8 48:9 52:15 Ps 19:4	Deut 32:21, 43 Isa 11:10 49:6 57:17 65:1 Hos 1:10 2:23 Amos 9:11–12 Ps 18:49 117:1	Deut 29:4 Isa 1:9 6:9–10 10:22–23 28:16 53:1 65:2 Ps 69:22–23

IV.

THE EXPECTATION THAT JESUS WILL COME AGAIN

On the basis of his resurrection the early Christians came to believe that Jesus was the Christ, despite his not having claimed to be the Christ, and despite his lack of resemblance to the Christ of contemporary expectation. This way of arriving at their faith left the early Christians with two problems. On the one hand it was necessary to support their claim that Jesus was the Christ by showing that he did fulfill the promises of the scriptures, even though that had not previously been noticed. In this, as we have just seen, the early Christians were very successful.

However, this still left them with the problem of explaining how Jesus was the Christ, i.e., how he did the work of the Christ. The Christ expected by first-century Jews would have done the work of the Christ by destroying the enemies of Israel and establishing a righteous world order under God. But Jesus differed from what had been expected of the Christ on precisely this point. How could it be made credible that despite appearances Jesus actually did the work of the Christ? This has been the central theological problem for Christianity from the beginning. It is the need to solve this problem that most of all explains why his followers used so many titles for Jesus; they were necessary to explicate how Jesus was the Christ. It also explains why, right up to the present, Christians continue to try to explain what it means to say that Jesus is the Christ; it is an affirmation which requires further explanation.

The earliest and most important resolution of this problem was the expectation that Jesus would come a second time and then do all that the Christ had been expected to do. This was a simple and elegant explanation of how Jesus was the Christ. It required minimal adjustment of expectation of the Christ and provided a simple way in which Jesus would fulfill that expectation. He had not done so at his first coming, but would at his second. This is still a fundamental article of Christian faith.

But where did the early Christians get this idea? It is conceivable that it was simply a solution to a theological problem. Or it might have derived from interpretation of scripture. After the early Christians succeeded in finding passages which predicted the kind of Christ Jesus turned out to be, there remained the other passages which had previously been seen as predicting a glorious, conquering Christ. One way to explain the existence of two groups of passages, both referring to the Christ but in very different terms, would be to suppose that they referred to two different comings of the Christ.[1] Both of these may have contributed to the development of the expectation that Jesus would come again. But a crucial factor was probably what Jesus had said about the son of man.

1. Son of Man[2]

It is curious that this title, which is very common in sayings of Jesus, is found in the rest of the New Testament, apart from Old Testament quotations and allusions, only in Acts 7:56.[3] This probably means that, even though the gospels are among the later New Testament writings, the

title 'son of man' goes back to Jesus and his earliest followers. If the presence of this title in the gospels were a result
of later influences, we would expect to find traces of it
elsewhere.

Likewise, the evangelists themselves do not express
their faith in Jesus by using this title. No doubt they think
it says something important about Jesus when it occurs in
the sayings of Jesus which they record. But when they
speak of Jesus in their own voice, they do not call him 'son
of man.' It is possible that the term 'son of man' in the sayings of Jesus simply reflects Jesus' use of it. But it is more
likely that it also reflects an understanding of Jesus on the
part of those who transmitted these sayings orally.
However, this understanding of Jesus, at least as
expressed by the term 'son of man,' had dropped into the
background by the time the writings of the New
Testament were produced.

The main reason for this may be linguistic. The term
'son of man' embodies one use of the expression 'son of'
that is peculiar to Semitic languages, namely its use to
indicate membership in a group or class. 'Man' in this
phrase means 'human being.' Thus 'son of man' means
'member of the human race' or simply 'human being.'
When Jesus spoke of the 'son of man' and when his earliest followers repeated what he said, presumably in
Aramaic or Hebrew, this meaning of the term was clear.
But when the term was translated literally into Greek, its
meaning was no longer clear because Greek (like English)
lacks the special usage embodied in the term. Therefore,
when the early Christians proclaimed Jesus to the Greek-
speaking world, and when Greek-speaking Christians produced the writings of the New Testament, they did not
speak of Jesus as 'son of man.' However, they did continue
to repeat sayings of Jesus about the 'son of man,' perhaps
because of a wish to preserve them unchanged.

Many scholars suppose that first-century Jews were expecting an eschatological figure called the 'son of man' much as they were expecting an eschatological figure called the Christ.[4] Others argue that this is not so. In the first century 'Christ' had become a technical term; the word in itself, in many contexts, would evoke a well-defined eschatological figure. But this was not true of 'son of man.' The only context in which it would reliably evoke a well-defined eschatological figure would be when Dan 7:13 was in view.[5]

I think the latter view is more likely to be true. For one thing, apart from the New Testament, the main evidence that 'son of man' was a technical term for an eschatological figure is the similitudes of 1 *Enoch*. However, this part of the text is missing from the Hebrew and Greek versions and is found only in the Ethiopic version. This may indicate that the section is a late addition to the writing. For another, the Dead Sea Scrolls show that in the first century 'son of man' continued to be used in other ways than to refer to an eschatological figure.[6]

Daniel 7 recounts a vision in which Daniel first sees four beasts (vv 3–8); then he sees the Ancient One judge the four beasts (vv 9–12) and give dominion to "one like a son of man" (vv 13–14). This vision is interpreted in vv 17–18. The four beasts and the "one like a son of man" are symbolic figures. The beasts represent four kingdoms; the "one like a son of man" represents the holy ones of the Most High. He is described as "one like a son of man" to indicate that he is human in appearance, unlike the four beasts. The holy ones of the Most High are probably the faithful people of Israel.

It is clear that by the first century Daniel 7:13 was understood as referring to an individual who would play a part in the final judgment. However, it seems likely that the 'son of man' had not become an expected figure in

people's minds such that even when they were not thinking of Daniel 7:13 they would understand the term as
referring to that figure. It was only when Daniel 7:13 was
in view that 'son of man' would have this meaning. At
other times 'son of man' would have its ordinary sense in
Hebrew or Aramaic.

Jesus' Son of Man Sayings

There are many passages in the gospels in which Jesus
says something about the son of man.[7] The authenticity of
these sayings and their meaning are vigorously debated.
While some scholars argue that all son of man sayings were
created by the early church,[8] most see at least some of Jesus'
son of man sayings as authentic. Some of those who take
the latter position argue that only the sayings about the
future activity of the son of man are authentic. These are
seen either as Jesus' references to himself[9] or as references to
someone else.[10] Others argue that it is mainly the sayings
about the present activity of the son of man that are authentic.[11] Still others argue that some sayings of both types are
authentic; these are seen as Jesus' references to himself.[12] In
agreement with most scholars I regard at least some of
Jesus' son of man sayings as authentic. I further assume that
the pattern of the sayings included in the gospels reflects
the pattern of Jesus' authentic sayings. While we cannot be
sure that any given saying derives from Jesus, we can at
least deduce the way he spoke about the son of man from
the way he is said to have spoken.

(a) Jesus' Son of Man Sayings and Daniel 7:13

In some of these sayings of Jesus the 'son of man' he
refers to is clearly the figure of Dan 7:13. For example, in

Mark 13:26 and parallels Jesus says, "Then they will see the Son of man coming in the clouds with great power and glory."[13]

On the other hand, 'son of man' in many sayings of Jesus does not seem to refer to the figure mentioned in Dan 7:13. This is true first of all in sayings where 'son of man' seems to have no content. For example, in Matt 16:13–15 Jesus asks his disciples, "Who do men say that the Son of man is?" The disciples respond, "Some say John the Baptist, others say Elijah, and others Jeremiah or one of the prophets." Then Jesus asks, "Who do you say that I am?" This exchange presupposes that 'son of man' is equivalent to 'I' and communicates nothing about the person called the 'son of man,' certainly not that he is the one mentioned in Dan 7:13. The person called 'son of man' must be further identified as John or a prophet.[14]

Secondly, 'son of man' does not seem to refer to the figure mentioned in Dan 7:13 in sayings in which Jesus says something about the 'son of man' which is not related to the description in Daniel 7. For example, in Mark 2:10 and parallels Jesus says that "the Son of man has authority on earth to forgive sins." In Matt 8:20 and parallel Jesus says that "the Son of man has nowhere to lay his head."[15]

Thirdly and most emphatically, 'son of man' does not seem to refer to the figure mentioned in Dan 7:13 in sayings in which Jesus speaks about the suffering and death of the 'son of man.' This seems to have no relationship to the 'son of man' of Dan 7:13. In passages like Mark 14:21 and parallels Jesus speaks of the betrayal of the 'son of man.' In Mark 8:31 and parallel, and many other passages, Jesus predicts the suffering and death of the 'son of man.' In John, Jesus says that the 'son of man' will be lifted up.[16] This refers to crucifixion, although crucifixion is seen as the first stage in being lifted up to rejoin the Father.

(b) Jesus' Son of Man Sayings and Himself

In some sayings it is fairly clear that 'son of man' refers to Jesus himself. This is clearest in a passage like Matt 16:13 where 'son of man' is equivalent to 'I.' But it is also fairly clear in Mark 2:10 and parallels where Jesus, having forgiven the sins of the paralytic, says that he will show the bystanders that the 'son of man' has authority to forgive sins by healing the paralytic. It also seems clear in Mark 14:21 and parallels where Jesus, after speaking of his own betrayal, talks about the betrayal of the 'son of man.'

However, in many sayings it is possible that 'son of man' refers to someone other than Jesus. This possibility results largely from the fact that 'son of man' is grammatically third person and would most naturally refer to someone other than the speaker in any saying. No doubt the evangelists understand 'son of man' as referring to Jesus every time it occurs, and this interpretation is always possible. But considered in themselves, many of these sayings can be seen as references to someone other than Jesus. And in some cases, this even seems most likely to be the original meaning of the saying. For example, in Luke 18:8 Jesus asks, "When the Son of man comes, will he find faith on earth?" Jesus could be referring to himself, but it would be most natural to see this as a reference to someone else.

Further, 'son of man' most clearly refers to Jesus in sayings where it does not seem to refer to the figure mentioned in Dan 7:13. And conversely, 'son of man' seems least likely to refer to Jesus where it does seem to refer to the figure mentioned in Dan 7:13.

(c) The Meaning of Son of Man for Jesus

One way to account for this is to suppose that Jesus used 'son of man' in two different ways.[17] Sometimes he

used it to refer to himself, with a meaning equivalent to 'I.'
In doing so he might either have been coining his own
term for himself, or making use of an idiom according to
which 'son of man' was a circumlocution for 'I.' At a later
time this was an established usage in Aramaic; it is not yet
certain that this was already so in the first century.[18] When
Jesus used 'son of man' in this way, he simply spoke about
himself; he intended no allusion to the figure mentioned
in Dan 7:13.

However, at other times Jesus used 'son of man' in
order to speak of the figure mentioned in Dan 7:13. In
these cases it is not clear whether Jesus identifies himself
with that figure or not. But it is clear that Jesus sees a close
connection between himself and that figure. For example,
in Mark 8:38 and parallel Jesus says, "For whoever is
ashamed of me and of my words in this adulterous and
sinful generation, of him will the Son of man also be
ashamed, when he comes in the glory of his Father with
the holy angels." It seems fairly clear that 'son of man'
here refers to the figure mentioned in Dan 7:13. It is not
clear whether 'son of man' refers to Jesus or not, though
the latter might seem more likely. But what is entirely clear
is that one's reaction to Jesus determines the reaction one
will receive from the 'son of man.' If someone is ashamed
of Jesus, the 'son of man' will also be ashamed of him or
her. If Jesus is not the 'son of man,' at least his mission is
intimately connected to the coming of the 'son of man.'[19]

(d) The Meaning of Son of Man for the Early Church

After the death and resurrection of Jesus, his followers understood all of his sayings about the 'son of man' as
references to himself, and saw Jesus as the figure mentioned in Dan 7:13. Since some of Jesus' sayings about the
'son of man' unambiguously referred to himself, and some

unambiguously referred to Dan 7:13, this must have seemed the obvious interpretation of the sayings as a whole. We can easily understand this because it still seems the obvious interpretation to the casual reader of the New Testament.

However, this understanding of Jesus' 'son of man' sayings also contributed to the explanation of how Jesus did the work of the Christ.[20] As we have seen, one of the passages that was understood as a prediction of the resurrection of Jesus was Ps 110:1. In the light of this passage, Jesus' resurrection was seen as his enthronement at the right hand of God in heaven. Seeing Jesus as the 'son of man' mentioned in Dan 7:13 made possible a further interpretation of this enthronement. Daniel 7:9 says that thrones were set up and that the Ancient One took his seat on one of them. Verses 13–14 speak of the coming of one like a son of man to the Ancient One to receive dominion and glory and kingdom. It seems clearly implied that the one like a son of man sat on the other throne. Thus the enthronement of Ps 110:1 could also be seen as the enthronement of the 'son of man' implied in Dan 7. And this would explain how Jesus did the work of the Christ because the enthronement of the son of man is at the same time the establishment of the kingdom of God.

Thus the earliest explanation of how Jesus did the work of the Christ may have been that his resurrection was the coming of the son of man to the Ancient One described in Dan 7, establishing the kingdom of God. This view may be expressed in Luke 22:69 where Jesus says, "But from now on the Son of man shall be seated at the right hand of the power of God."[21] However, it must very quickly have become obvious that the kingdom of God had not simply arrived with the resurrection of Jesus. In response to this, the early Christians may have revised their understanding to allow for Jesus' assumption of eschatological sovereignty in the future. He was the 'son of man' but his coming to the Ancient One to inaugurate the kingdom of God still lay in the future. This idea that Jesus would assume full sovereignty in the future was the earliest form of the belief that Jesus would come again.

The chief expression of this view is found in Mark 14:62 and Matt 26:64. Having been asked if he is the Christ, Jesus says, "I am; and you will see the Son of man sitting at the right hand of Power, and coming with the clouds of heaven." In the first half of the verse we find the combination of Ps 110:1 and Dan 7:13 which interprets Jesus' resurrection as the enthronement of the 'son of man.' I suggest that the latter part of the verse is an addition intended to distinguish between Jesus' enthronement as son of man and his later coming with the clouds of heaven, presumably at the end of the world. It is not clear whether this coming with the clouds is understood as Jesus' coming to the Ancient One to be enthroned, or as his coming from heaven to earth. But on either understanding the picture of the 'son of man' enthroned and then coming is awkward. This may be another reason, in addition to the linguistic reason already mentioned, why the belief that Jesus would come again is usually not expressed in terms of the future coming of the son of man outside of the gospel tradition. Despite its importance in the development of that belief, talk about Jesus as 'son of man' was not a very apt vehicle for expressing the expectation that he would come again. The sayings of Jesus included many which mentioned the 'son of man,' and these continued to be understood in light of the expectation of his second coming. But apart from sayings of Jesus, this belief was expressed in other terms, especially in terms of Jesus as lord.

2. Lord[22]

The expectation that Jesus would come again was not simply the result of identifying Jesus the Christ with the 'son of man' of Daniel 7. Another significant factor was further reflection on Ps 110:1 and on Jesus as lord.

Use of the title 'lord' (= Aramaic *mar*; Hebrew *adon*; Greek *kyrios*) for someone is an acknowledgment of the rightful authority of a superior over an inferior. Thus in the Old Testament 'lord' is frequently used as a title for the leaders of Israel—priests, prophets, and most of all, kings—and as a title for God.

'Lord' is the second most common title for Jesus in the New Testament, though it is absent from Titus and 1–3 John. The title is frequently given to Jesus in the gospels. In part this reflects the later faith of his followers that Jesus is lord. However, it seems quite likely that Jesus was called lord during his lifetime. In the gospels Jesus is called lord by those who are asking for his help[23] and by his disciples.[24] It seems entirely likely that both of these groups would acknowledge his authority by calling him lord.

An even more important reason for the early church's use of 'lord' as a title for Jesus was their faith that he was the Christ. The Christ was the eschatological king; the king is one of those for whom the title 'lord' is most appropriate.[25] Use of the title 'lord' for Jesus as Christ is founded above all on the interpretation of Ps 110:1 as applying to him. This psalm originally applied to the king of Israel. The psalmist begins, "The Lord [i.e., God] says to my lord [i.e., the king]." When this psalm was understood as a prediction fulfilled by Jesus the Christ, it was also seen as implying that Jesus is lord. A connection between Ps 110:1 and the title 'lord' is visible in Mark 12:35–37 and parallels. Here Jesus asks how the Christ can be David's son when David calls him lord.[26]

We have already seen that in combination with Dan 7:13, Ps 110:1 was used to interpret Jesus' resurrection as the enthronement of the son of man and the establishment of the kingdom of God. When it became necessary to adjust this view to speak of Jesus' assumption of full sovereignty in the future, Ps 110:1 provided further help. This verse describes the enthronement of the Christ as being "till I make your enemies your footstool." This could easily be seen as implying that there would be an interval between the enthronement of the Christ and the subjection of his enemies, i.e., his assumption of full sovereignty.

The New Testament passage which most directly presents such an interpretation of Ps 110:1 is Heb 10:12–13. This passage clearly interprets the resurrection of Jesus as the fulfillment of the session at God's right hand mentioned in Ps 110:1, and goes on to speak of an interval until Jesus' enemies shall be made his footstool, an interval probably concluded by a second appearance of Jesus.[27] This interpretation of Ps 110:1 may also underlie Col 3:1–4. Here Jesus is envisioned as sitting at God's right hand, presumably since his resurrection; after some interval he will reappear, an interval which may be an interpretation of "till I make your enemies your footstool" in Ps 110:1. This interpretation of the psalm is clear in Justin, *Apol.* 45.[28]

Thus we see that on the basis of Ps 110:1 Jesus was seen as the lord enthroned in heaven awaiting the time when his enemies would be subjected to him. The final stage in the full development of the expectation that Jesus would come again occurred when Old Testament passages which speak about the coming of the lord were interpreted as referring to the lord Jesus. For example, Zech 14:5 says, "Then the Lord your God will come, and all the holy ones with him." Alluding to this passage, 1 Thess 3:13 speaks of "the coming of our Lord Jesus with all his saints." At least partly on the basis of use of the title 'lord' for Jesus, the

Old Testament passage, which originally referred to the Lord God, has been seen as referring to Jesus. Understood in this way, the Old Testament passage presents the now familiar idea of a second coming of Jesus and gives details of this coming, telling us that he will be accompanied by his saints.[29]

The earliest expression of hope for the second coming of the Lord Jesus is the Aramaic prayer *marana tha* (= Our Lord, come).[30] This prayer is found in the Greek text of 1 Cor 16:22 and *Didache* 10.6.[31] This is probably a prayer used in the earliest Aramaic-speaking church and retained in the Greek-speaking churches to which Paul writes and from which the *Didache* derives. This prayer was probably used in the Christian celebration of the Lord's Supper. It requests the second coming of the Lord (= Jesus, the Christ), and his anticipatory presence among his followers as they celebrate the Lord's Supper.

3. Son of God[32]

We have seen that the expectation that Jesus will come again arose when Ps 110:1 was first connected with Dan 7:13 and later connected with Old Testament passages that spoke about the coming of the Lord. Because of this, hope for the second coming of Jesus is expressed in terms of Jesus as son of man in the gospel tradition, and in terms of Jesus as lord elsewhere. However, this hope is also expressed in other terms. In at least one passage it is expressed in terms of hope for the return of Jesus the son of God. In 1 Thess 1:9–10 Paul says that the Thessalonians "serve a living and true God" and "wait for his Son from heaven, whom he raised from the dead, Jesus who delivers us from the wrath to come." It does not seem that understanding Jesus as son of God contributed anything to the development of the expectation that Jesus would come again. But after Jesus was seen as son of God on other grounds, this hope could also be expressed in terms of his being son of God.

In Semitic languages the expression 'son of' indicates a relationship, but not exclusively or even primarily that of physical descent. Thus, in the Old Testament many persons are called 'sons of God' in order to indicate their special relationship with God. The title is applied to members of the heavenly court, or angels, to the people of Israel, and to the king of Israel. Jesus is frequently presented as son of God in the New Testament. In the gospels Jesus calls God his father[33] and less often refers to himself as son or son of God. To some extent this presentation of Jesus as saying that he was the son of God undoubtedly reflects the later belief of his followers that he was son of God. But that the historical Jesus spoke of God as his father is very likely. One thing that supports this is the presence of *abba*, an Aramaic word meaning father, in the Greek text of Mark 14:36. This may go back to the historical Jesus and perhaps because of that was used by Greek-speaking Christians.[34]

It is not clear what self-understanding is implied by Jesus' use of 'father' for God and 'son' for himself. In the gospels Jesus also frequently calls God the father of those to whom he is speaking.[35] It is possible that Jesus regarded himself as son of God in the same sense that many others were children of God. On the other hand, some passages suggest that Jesus saw himself as son of God in a unique sense. Most important is Matt 11:25–27/Luke 10:21–22. Here Jesus says, "No one knows the Son except the Father, and no one knows the Father except the Son and any one to whom the Son chooses to reveal him." In addition, an understanding of Jesus as son of God in a unique sense pervades the gospel of John.[36] In the light of this it seems possible that Jesus saw himself as Son of God in the sense that he had a special mission to reveal God to the world.[37]

An even more important reason for the early church's use of the title 'son of God' for Jesus was their faith that he was the Christ.[38] The Christ was the eschatological king; the king was one of those called son of God.[39] Use of the title 'son of God' for Jesus as Christ was based especially on two passages. The first is Ps 2:7—"You are my son, today I have begotten you"—originally addressed to the king of Israel. The second is 2 Sam 7:14. Here the prophet Nathan, speaking for God, promises David concerning his offspring, "I will be his father, and he shall be my son." This passage is seen as applying to the Christ in 4QFlor, which quotes 2 Sam 7:14 and explains that it refers to the shoot of David, i.e., the Christ, "who will appear…in Zion at the end of days" [my translation]. When these passages were seen as fulfilled by Jesus the Christ, they were also seen as implying that Jesus was son of God. Having referred to Jesus as son of God in 1:2, Heb 1:5 quotes both of these passages. The equivalence of Christ and son of God is clear in several New Testament passages. In Matt 16:16 Peter confesses that Jesus is "the Christ, the Son of the living God." In Mark 14:61/Matt 26:63 the high priest asks Jesus, "Are you the Christ, the Son of the Blessed?"[40]

Because in its earliest use 'son of God' is practically synonymous with 'Christ,' Jesus could be called the son of God who would come again simply as an alternative to speaking of the Christ who would come again. This seems to be what underlies 1 Thess 1:9–10.

4. Expressions of This Belief

The expectation that Jesus will come again is found in most of the writings of the New Testament, though never as a complete explanation of how Jesus did the work of the Christ. It is always combined with one or both of the other explanations we will discuss in Chapters VI and VII.

In the letters of Paul we find three notable discussions of the expectation that Jesus will come again. In 1 Thess 4:13–5:11 Paul exhorts the Thessalonians not to grieve over the dead because the dead will rise when Jesus comes again. Paul then goes on to urge them to live as is appropriate for those who know that the Lord is coming. In 2 Thess 2:1–12 (perhaps not written by Paul), the Thessalonians are exhorted not to be too quickly excited about the coming of Jesus because it will be preceded by various signs that have not yet occurred. And in 1 Cor 15:20–28 Paul outlines the course of events from the resurrection of Jesus to his second coming, as he tries to persuade the Corinthians to affirm the resurrection of the dead.

In the synoptic gospels expectation of Jesus' second coming is especially expressed in Jesus' eschatological discourse (Mark 13 and parallels). In the course of a detailed presentation of the events of the end times, Jesus says that the son of man will come (Mark 13:26 and parallels). As we have seen, it is very likely that the evangelists understand this as Jesus' prediction of his own return.

2 Peter 3:3–13 is an attempt to respond to those who doubt that Jesus will come again. The author counters the argument that nothing ever changes by pointing to the precedent of the flood (vv 4–7). The author explains the delay in Jesus' return as a result of the different meaning of time for God and for humans (v 8) and as an opportunity for repentance (v 9). Finally, the readers are urged to live as is appropriate for those awaiting the day of the Lord (vv 11–13).

The New Testament document for which expectation of the second coming of Jesus is most central is the book of

Revelation. The whole message of Revelation is that its readers should remain faithful to Jesus, despite the difficulty of doing so, because he is coming soon. The first verse of Revelation sums up its content as an account of "what must soon take place" (1:1). And the central element of this is expressed a few verses later: "Behold, [Jesus] is coming with the clouds" (1:7). This summary of content is repeated at the end of Revelation (22:6–7, 20). In between lies a detailed description of the events of the end time in symbolic terms (6:1–20:6), concluding with the second coming of Jesus. Jesus is pictured as a warrior on a white horse who will conquer the forces of evil and reign for a thousand years with those who have been faithful to him (19:11–20:6).

Summary

Thus far we have been examining the first and most basic explanation of how Jesus did the work of the Christ, namely the idea that he would come again. I have proposed that this idea arose when Jesus' resurrection was seen not only as the fulfillment of Ps 110:1, but also as the enthronement of the son of man mentioned in Dan 7:13, partly on the basis of what Jesus had said about the son of man. Seeing Jesus' resurrection as the enthronement of the son of man meant understanding it as leading immediately to the establishment of the kingdom of God. When that did not happen, it became necessary to look for Jesus' assumption of full sovereignty in the future. This was the earliest form of the expectation that Jesus would come again.

Initially this was expressed in terms of the future coming of the son of man. But partly because it was not easy to express this idea on the basis of the combination of

Ps 110:1 and Dan 7:13, the idea was further developed by means of reflection on Ps 110:1 alone and the confession of Jesus as lord. This encouraged the early Christians to see Old Testament passages which spoke about the coming of the lord as applying to the lord Jesus. At this point the expectation that Jesus would come again was fully developed.

As a result of this development, Jesus' followers spoke of him as the Christ who would come again,[41] as the son of man who would come in glory (though for linguistic and other reasons this usage ceased among Greek-speaking Christians except in the gospel tradition), and as the lord who would come again. In addition the expectation that Jesus would come again could be expressed in terms of the title 'son of God' because it was seen as equivalent to 'Christ.'

All of this is summed up in Mark 14:61–62. The high priest asked Jesus, "Are you the Christ, the son of the Blessed?" Jesus answered, "I am; and you will see the son of man sitting at the right hand of Power, and coming with the clouds of heaven." We also find this expectation expressed in other ways throughout the New Testament.

V.

JESUS' DEATH AS ATONEMENT[1]

If Jesus will do the work of the Christ by coming a second time to establish the kingdom of God, it remains to be asked what is the significance of his life, death and resurrection. And clearly the item most urgently in need of explanation was the death of Jesus. I do not mean to imply that this question arose only after the development of the expectation that Jesus would come again.[2] Even those whose focus was showing that Jesus was the Christ by showing that he fulfilled scripture might have asked about the meaning of his death. But obviously, an explanation of how Jesus does the work of the Christ which looks mainly to the future and to something Jesus has not yet done raises the question of the meaning of the past very forcefully.

It seems that the earliest explanation of the death of Jesus was that it was an atonement for sin. Understood in this way the death of Jesus prepares for his second coming by giving people a means of freedom from sin. This allows them to be among the elect who will be saved at the second coming. This understanding of the death of Jesus was probably based both on the ideology of sacrifice[3] and on the idea of the atoning significance of the death of martyrs.[4] But in addition it was based on identifying Jesus with other ideas and figures in terms of which his death could be seen as atoning. We will look at four.[5]

1. Suffering Servant[6]

A number of scholars have seen the idea that Jesus was the suffering servant of God as the key to Jesus' self-understanding and to the origin of Christian faith.[7] Others see it as much less significant.[8] The former see the idea that Jesus was the suffering servant as the solution to the problem which we have earlier discussed at length (see Chapter II above). They argue that the early Christians believed in Jesus as the Christ even though he differed greatly from the expected Christ, because they also saw him as the suffering servant. Since I have already given a different explanation of early Christian faith in Jesus as Christ (see Chapter III above), I see no need for the idea that he was the suffering servant to provide this key explanation. Thus I align myself with the latter group of scholars.

When scholars consider the idea that Jesus was the suffering servant of God, they have in mind that he saw himself, or was seen, as the fulfillment of four passages in Isaiah.[9] They combine all citations of, or allusions to, these passages in arguing that Jesus was the suffering servant of God. However, it is only the last two of these passages which speak of a suffering servant, and only the last explicitly says that this suffering was an atonement, an element usually presumed to be part of the idea of the suffering servant. And there is no reason to suppose that in the first century these four passages were seen as connected. Modern scholarship has isolated and linked them, but in the first century these passages were simply seen as parts of the book of Isaiah. Thus it is only legitimate to see the idea of a suffering servant where there is a citation of, or allusion to, the fourth passage, i.e., Isa 52:13–53:12. Citations of, or allusions to, the other passages do not imply the idea of a suffering servant, nor does the term 'servant' itself, which is found elsewhere in the book of Isaiah and throughout the Old Testament.

It is sometimes argued that Jesus' predictions of his own death imply that he saw himself as the suffering servant of God. While many scholars have argued that these predictions are not authentic sayings of Jesus, I see no reason to doubt that Jesus foresaw his own death, though the present form of the sayings may have been influenced by subsequent events. However, even if Jesus did predict his own death, this does not imply that he saw himself as the one spoken about in Isa 52:13–53:12. It could have been his assessment of what was likely to happen to him without any reference to fulfillment of scripture at all. Or, as we will see, it might have been connected with an understanding of himself as a prophet.

One saying of Jesus quotes Isa 52:13–53:12, and it has been argued that two others allude to it. These sayings are the basis on which it can be argued that Jesus saw himself as the suffering servant of God. In Luke 22:37, just before he is arrested Jesus says, "For I tell you that this scripture must be fulfilled in me, 'And he was reckoned with transgressors' (Isa 53:12); for what is written about me has its fulfillment." This saying is unique to Luke and is thus absent from the earliest collections of Jesus' sayings, i.e., Mark and Q. And as we have seen, the early Christians tried to show that Jesus was the fulfillment of scripture; we might wonder if this saying reflects that effort rather than Jesus' own consciousness. But even if the saying is genuine, it need not mean that Jesus saw all of Isa 52:13–53:12 as applying to him. He might have meant only that the clause he actually quotes applied to him. And this would interpret his arrest, etc., as putting him among transgressors; it need not mean that he saw it as atoning.

One passage that has been seen as an allusion to Isa 52:13–53:12 is Mark 10:45/Matt 20:28. Here Jesus says that the Son of man came "to give his life as a ransom for many." Similarly, in Mark 14:24 and parallels, as he gives his disciples the cup at the Last Supper Jesus says, "This is my blood of the covenant, which is poured out for many." The reference to Jesus' death as a death 'for many' certainly corresponds to the description of the suffering servant in Isa 52:13–53:12. However, it does not seem that these words necessarily derive from this passage or refer to it.[10]

Thus it seems to me unlikely that Jesus saw himself as the suffering servant of God. However, it is certain that the early church did see him this way. This was probably not an understanding which followed simply from believing that Jesus was the Christ. Although the references to the servant in Isa 52:13–53:12 were understood as references to the Christ in Jewish interpretation, the idea of suffering as atonement for the many was never attached to the Christ.[11] The early church probably identified Jesus as the suffering servant because this provided an explanation of Jesus' death which was otherwise mysterious. It was a sacrificial death suffered on behalf of others.

This interpretation of Jesus' death is reflected in Rom 4:25 where Paul says that Jesus "was put to death for our trespasses." This alludes to Isa 53:12. Hebrews 9:28 also alludes to this passage. Interpretation of Jesus' death as a fulfillment of Isa 52:13–53:12 is clearest of all in Acts 8:32–35 and 1 Pet 2:22–25. As we have already noted (see Chapter III above), in both of these passages Isa 53 is quoted and said to have been fulfilled by Jesus' death. In the Acts passage Isa 52:13–53:12 is not explicitly used to interpret Jesus' death as atoning. However, this interpretation is found in the passage from 1 Peter. Because Isa 52:13–53:12 seems to correspond closely to our understanding of Jesus' death, it is surprising that the early church did not make more use of this passage to interpret

Jesus' death as atoning. But for some reason the early church did not mainly look to this passage, at least not explicitly, in order to present Jesus' death as atoning.

2. Prophet[12]

A second idea that was applied to Jesus in order to explain his death as atonement was the idea that he was a prophet. Identification of Jesus as a prophet helped to explain his death because of the widespread first-century view that prophets inevitably met with death. For example, in 1 Thess 2:15 Paul says that the Jews "killed…the prophets."[13] Such passages do not say, as Isa 52:13–53:12 does, that death is suffered for the sake of others. However, this seems to be implied. The mission of the prophet is to benefit others; the prophet is killed as a result of carrying out that mission; and in that sense the death of the prophet is for others. It is a death suffered as a result of acting on behalf of others.

The idea that Jesus was a prophet rests on several different foundations. One is that Jesus resembled a prophet. His ministry consisted of teaching and working miracles, and these are the main activities of a prophet. This can be seen clearly in the careers of Elijah and Elisha, narrated in the books of Kings. And as we have just seen, Jesus could also be said to resemble a prophet in his death.

A second foundation for the idea that Jesus was a prophet is that Jesus may have referred to himself as a prophet. In Mark 6:4 and parallels Jesus applies to himself the proverb, "A prophet is not without honor, except in his own country." In Luke 13:33 Jesus says that he must travel to Jerusalem because "it cannot be that a prophet should perish away from Jerusalem." If these sayings make it likely that Jesus referred to himself as a prophet, there is little indication that the claim to be a prophet was at all central to his teaching. However, it is intrinsically the most likely category in which Jesus might have understood himself.[14]

A third foundation for the idea that Jesus was a prophet is that in the first century Jews were expecting an eschatological prophet to appear.[15] When Jesus was seen as the Christ, he was also seen as the eschatological prophet, partly because it was considered appropriate that a king, and thus the Christ, also be a prophet. We see evidence of this in John 6:14–15. After people saw Jesus' multiplication of loaves and fish, they said, "This is indeed the prophet who is to come into the world." Then the narrator comments that Jesus perceived that the people would try to "make him king."[16]

The expectation of an eschatological prophet arose in much the same way as did the expectation of the Christ. In both cases reflection on scripture in the light of history led to an eschatological expectation. In Deut 18:15 Moses says, "The Lord your God will raise up for you a prophet like me from among you." And in Mal 4:5 it says, "Behold, I will send you Elijah the prophet before the great and terrible day of the Lord comes." By the first century it seemed that prophets had long ago ceased to be sent to Israel. And so people looked for the fulfillment of passages like these in the sending of an eschatological prophet. And this expectation took two main forms: expectation of a prophet like Moses and expectation of Elijah.

We find expressions of this expectation in the Qumran literature. In 1QS 9.10–11 there is reference to remaining faithful to the precepts of the community until the coming of the prophet. And in 4QTestim, Deut 18:18–19 is quoted, apparently in reference to this expected prophet. We find other expressions of this expectation in the New Testament. Mark 6:14 and parallels reports that some people said Jesus was Elijah, while others said that he was a prophet like one of the prophets of old.[17] According to John 1:21 there was similar speculation about John the Baptist. There is further reference to the expected coming of Elijah in Mark 9:11 and parallels. And in several passages John the Baptist is said to fulfill the expectation that Elijah will come again.[18]

There is no explicit indication that this eschatological prophet was expected to die. But it would have been easy to add this element to the picture of the eschatological prophet because death was seen as the common fate of all prophets. This step is taken most clearly by Luke-Acts. In Luke 13:33 Jesus' journey to Jerusalem, which extends from Luke 9:51 to 19:28, is interpreted as the journey of a prophet to die in Jerusalem. Acts 7:52 parallels the killing of the prophets and the killing of Jesus. Seeing Jesus not only as the Christ, but also as eschatological prophet allows Luke to explain the death of Jesus as a death suffered for others as he carried out his mission on their behalf.

3. Son of God

We have already seen that Jesus was called Son of God both because of the way he spoke about himself as Son of God during his lifetime and because as the Christ he was Son of God. We have also seen that he was called Son of God in connection with the expectation that he would come again. One passage reflects use of the idea that Jesus was Son of God to explain his death as an atoning death.

In Rom 8:32 Paul says that God "did not spare his own Son but gave him up for us all." This alludes to Gen 22:16–17 where God tells Abraham that "because you...have not withheld your son, your only son, I will indeed bless you." N. A. Dahl has argued that this allusion reflects the view that the death of Jesus is a fulfillment of God's promise to Abraham, which is commensurate with that on which the promise was based. God made the promise because Abraham was willing to sacrifice his son. In fulfilling the promise God actually sacrifices his son Jesus. Thus the death of Jesus is a sacrifice, as the death of Isaac would have been if it had gone that far. And this sacrifice brings the blessing which God promised Abraham. In Dahl's words, the atonement is an adequate reward for the *akedah* (i.e., the binding of Isaac).[19]

Paul does not develop this idea explicitly or put any emphasis on it. But the allusion seems to show the existence of an understanding of the death of Jesus as atoning which antedates the composition of Romans and may be a very early theological idea.

4. Priest[20]

A fourth idea in terms of which the death of Jesus could be seen as atoning was the idea that Jesus was a priest and his death a sacrifice which he offered as priest. Jesus was not a priest in ordinary Jewish terms; he lacked the essential qualification of belonging to the tribe of Levi and the family of Aaron. Nor did Jesus make any claim to be a priest, as far as we know. Therefore, the idea that Jesus was a priest is more mysterious than most of the other ideas in terms of which he was understood.

The main foundation for the idea that Jesus was a priest was first-century Jewish expectation of an eschatological priest. When Jesus was believed to be the Christ, he was also seen as the eschatological priest. One reason for this is that Ps 110 connects the two ideas. We have already seen that Ps 110:1 was understood as a passage which applied to Jesus as the Christ; it was seen as a prediction of his resurrection and his parousia. Verse 4 of the psalm says, "You are a priest for ever after the order of Melchizedek." This was understood as predicting that the Christ would also be a priest, a new kind of priest from the order of Melchizedek rather than from the tribe of Levi. This verse is explicitly cited several times in Hebrews.[21] It probably underlies Rom 8:34 where Jesus is said to be at the right hand of God, performing the priestly function of interceding for us.[22]

The expectation of an eschatological priest arose in much the same way as did the expectation of the Christ and the eschatological prophet. In all three cases reflection on scripture in the light of history led to an eschatological expectation. Passages like Num 25:12–13 express the promise of a perpetual righteous priesthood. But by the first century many saw the priesthood as corrupt. This was mainly because in the middle of the second century BCE the Hasmonean family had assumed the office of high priest, illegitimately from a strict point of view. The Hasmoneans were Levites, but not descendants of Zadok; according to some, only the latter could properly be high priests. This led to the expectation of an eschatological high priest who would restore the priesthood and fulfill the promises of scripture.

We find expressions of this expectation in the Qumran literature. 1QS 9.10–11 speaks of remaining faithful to the precepts of the community until the coming of the prophet and the Christs of Aaron and Israel. The Christ of Aaron is the eschatological priest; the Christ of Israel is the eschatological king usually meant by 'Christ.' Likewise 4QTestim cites Deut 18:18–19; Num 24:15–17; and Deut 33:8–11, apparently referring to the eschatological prophet, the eschatological king and the eschatological priest, respectively.[23] We also find this expectation in the *Testaments of the Twelve Patriarchs*.[24]

Naturally the eschatological priest was not expected to offer himself as a sacrifice. But the early Christians, confronted with a need to make sense of the crucifixion of Jesus, combined their belief that Jesus was the Christ with a belief that he was the eschatological priest, and explained his death as the sacrifice which he offered as priest. This is explicit in Heb 7:27, 10:10–14 and developed at greatest length in Heb 9. Here Jesus' sacrifice of himself is compared to the sacrifice offered on the day of atonement. The author of Hebrews argues that the sacrifice of Jesus accomplishes the intention of the sacrifice on the day of atonement completely so that there is no longer a need for an annual sacrifice.

Not only does Hebrews use the idea that Jesus is priest to explain the meaning of his death; for Hebrews, priesthood provides a comprehensive explanation of his career. The author of Hebrews is able to account for Jesus' life, death, resurrection and parousia within the framework of his being high priest.

Summary

Thus we see that the early Christians were able to interpret Jesus' death as atonement by linking him with two scriptural themes—the suffering servant and the Son of God—and by identifying him with two eschatological figures (in addition to the Christ)—the eschatological prophet and the eschatological priest.

These different ways of expressing the idea that Jesus' death was an atoning death imply different senses of atonement:

Suffering servant—vicarious death;

Prophet—death as a consequence of bringing God's word to others;

Son of God—death as appropriate fulfillment of promise to Abraham, a sign of great love;

Priest—death as sacrifice of oneself.

The interpretation of the death of Jesus as atonement continues to be basic to faith in Jesus as the Christ.

VI.

THE BELIEF THAT JESUS NOW REIGNS IN HEAVEN

1. The Influence of Hellenistic Culture

Thus far we have discussed how the early Christians came to believe that Jesus was the Christ, how they argued that scripture had predicted Jesus, how they explained that Jesus would do the work of the Christ when he came again, and how they explained the death of Jesus as an atoning death. All of this occurred among the earliest Palestinian Christians. Now we need to consider what happened as the Christian gospel was proclaimed and believed among people outside of Palestine.

I do not mean to suggest that prior to this Hellenistic culture had no influence on Christianity. As we have seen, the earliest faith in Jesus was a matter of seeing him as the fulfillment of apocalyptic expectations. And these apocalyptic expectations themselves were partly the result of the influence of Hellenistic culture on Judaism. However, the influence of Hellenistic culture was certainly different within Palestine than outside it. One indication of this is that apocalyptic expectation was widespread among first-century Palestinian Jews but not, as far as we know, among Jews living elsewhere. Though we cannot divide Palestinian and non-Palestinian Judaism completely, there was a difference between them with regard to the influence of Hellenistic culture.

I also do not mean to suggest that the spread of early Christianity outside of Palestine was a late development. Paul's persecution of Christians in Damascus implies that Christianity had spread to that city within two or three years of the death and resurrection of Jesus. And the Acts of the Apostles suggests that Christianity spread to Phoenicia, Cyprus and Antioch soon afterwards (Acts 11:19–26). The entire development described in this book took place within very few years.

A simple way to see the likely effect of the spread of the Christian gospel beyond Palestine is to consider that it probably involved translation from one language into another. In all probability the earliest Palestinian Christians spoke Aramaic or Hebrew or both.[1] Their verbal expressions of faith in Jesus would have been in that language. When they proclaimed their belief in Jesus outside of Palestine, they first had to translate verbal expressions into Greek, the language used almost everywhere in the Greco-Roman empire. Translation from one language into another also involves moving from the world in which the first is embedded into the world of the second. Inevitably translation involves losses and gains in meaning and thus changes what is translated.[2]

Thus the effect of the spread of the Christian gospel outside Palestine may well have been enormous. We will confine ourselves to considering its impact on some of the titles used for Jesus. This will allow us to sketch some of its most significant impact on the development of Christian faith. In general the spread of the Christian gospel outside of Palestine had two effects. It affected the selection of titles used for Jesus, and it affected the meaning of those titles.

(a) Selection of Titles

As we have seen, the most basic belief of the early Christians was that Jesus was the Christ. Literally 'Christ' means 'Anointed.' In Aramaic and Hebrew 'Anointed' had become the title of an expected savior, while in Greek it had not. Greek-speaking Jews do not seem to have had the lively expectation of the 'Anointed' that characterized some Aramaic and Hebrew-speaking Jews. Thus even for Greek-speaking Jews 'Christ' was not very meaningful. But for Gentiles 'Christ' simply meant 'anointed;' it did not at all suggest that the one so designated was a savior. We can readily appreciate this because it is also true for us. In twentieth-century English 'anointed' does not mean what it meant in first-century Palestine.

Of course, Greek-speaking Jews and Gentiles could be taught the meaning of 'Christ.' But in general the failure of Aramaic/Hebrew and Greek usage to match up at this point seems to have caused Christians to rely less on Christ to say who Jesus was to Greek-speakers, and more on other terms which were immediately meaningful. However, even if it was not the most useful term for expressing the meaning of Jesus to Greek-speakers, the belief that Jesus was the Christ was too basic to be abandoned. So Christ became in effect a second name for Jesus. Greek-speakers learned to call Jesus Christ even if they did not realize what it meant and mainly expressed their faith in him in other terms. Once again we can easily understand this because it is still true for us today.

On the other hand, the Greek equivalents of two of the titles used for Jesus, namely lord and Son of God, were widely used in Greek with a meaning relatively close to the meaning which they had in Aramaic and Hebrew. Because of this, these titles became more important as a way of expressing faith in Jesus to Greek-speakers.

However, because the meaning of the titles in Aramaic/Hebrew and Greek was only approximately, not exactly the same, use of the Greek titles for Jesus encouraged the development of faith in Jesus along certain lines.

(b) Change in the Meaning of Titles

We have seen that Jesus was called lord and Son of God because these titles were used for him during his lifetime, and even more because as the Christ he was also lord and Son of God. 'Lord' was an acknowledgement of his rightful authority as Christ; 'Son of God' expressed his special relationship with God as Christ.

The Greek equivalents of these titles meant much the same thing as the Aramaic/Hebrew originals. In Greek 'lord' was an expression of the rightful authority of a superior and was applied both to human beings and to gods. Likewise 'son of god' expressed a special relationship with the gods. The term was used for divine and semi-divine offspring of Zeus and other gods, for Roman emperors from Augustus onwards, meaning that they were the sons of the emperors who had preceded them and who had been divinized, and by the Stoics for all human beings since all shared in the divine reason which orders the cosmos.

However, these titles carried new overtones in Greek which they had not had in Aramaic/Hebrew. In Greek, Son of God suggested that Jesus had literally been begotten by God, something not implied by the title in Aramaic/Hebrew. And both terms suggested that Jesus was one of the large group of heavenly beings and divinities called lord and son of god in the Greek world. This tended to locate Jesus in the divine realm. The use of these titles in presenting Jesus to the Greek-speaking world contributed to an increasingly exalted view of Jesus.

This may have been true even for Greek-speaking Jewish Christians. As Jews they would not have believed in the many gods of the Gentile world. But living in the midst of Gentiles may have given terms like lord and Son of God new meaning even for them. Philo of Alexandria, as he attempts to relate the Jewish scriptures and Greek philosophy to one another, speaks of the *logos*, a divine being distinct from, but closely related to God. This *logos* he calls Son of God.[3] Philo also speaks of two powers by which God is manifested to human beings, the creative and the kingly. The latter is called lord.[4]

The early Christians made extensive use of the titles Son of God and especially lord in presenting their faith in Jesus to the world outside of Palestine, because these titles readily communicated roughly what they wanted to say about Jesus. However, use of these titles among Greek-speakers tended to locate Jesus in the divine realm. This the early Christians could embrace for reasons we will discuss below. But like non-Christian Jews in the Greek-speaking world, they rejected polytheism.

We can see Paul accepting some of the implications of calling Jesus lord and rejecting others in 1 Cor 8:5–6. "For although there may be so-called gods in heaven or on earth—as indeed there are many 'gods' and many 'lords'—yet for us there is one God, the Father, from whom are all things and for whom we exist, and one Lord, Jesus Christ, through whom are all things and through whom we exist." Calling Jesus lord puts him in the class of the many who are called lord, but for Christians there is only one real lord.

This Christian position would be problematic both for Jews and Gentiles. To Jews it would seem that acknowledging Jesus as lord and Son of God threatened belief in one God. To Gentiles it would seem inconsistent to affirm Jesus as lord and Son of God and to deny the existence of many gods. But early Christianity held firmly both to the faith that there was only one God, and to faith in Jesus as lord and Son of God. Ultimately this issued in the doctrine of the Trinity.

2. Development of Belief that Jesus Now Reigns in Heaven

Partly as a result of the proclamation of the Christian gospel outside of Palestine, the early Christians developed a second explanation of how Jesus did the work of the Christ. As we have seen, the earliest explanation of how Jesus did the work of the Christ was the expectation that he would come again; at his second coming he would do what was expected of the Christ. The new explanation of how Jesus did the work of the Christ was the belief that Jesus is now reigning in heaven. Not only will he establish the kingdom of God obviously and unmistakably at his second coming, he has already established it, though in a hidden way known only to believers. When Jesus' being the Christ is understood in this way, his life, death and resurrection are seen as a conquest of the spiritual powers of evil. Already he has secretly conquered the powers of evil and begun a new phase of world history.

This could function as an alternate explanation of how Jesus did the work of the Christ, replacing the expectation that Jesus will come again. Seen in this way, the salvation accomplished by Jesus would be entirely a present reality; nothing would remain to be accomplished in the future. Some early Christians may have understood Jesus this way, e.g., some in the Corinthian church established by Paul.[5] However, the authors of the New Testament writings that express this second explanation combine it with the first. They maintain that Jesus has already established the kingdom of God in one sense, but in another it remains to be fully established at Jesus' second coming. For them the salvation accomplished by Jesus is both a present reality and something to be completed in the future.

Similarly the understanding of Jesus' life, death and resurrection as a victory over the powers of evil could be an alternative to seeing it as atonement for sin. However, in the New Testament the two views are combined. Jesus' life, death and resurrection are seen both as atonement and as a victory.

(a) Sources of This Belief

The belief that Jesus presently reigns in heaven is a development of one of the earliest theological ideas of early Christianity, namely, that in fulfillment of Ps 110:1 Jesus' resurrection was his enthronement at God's right hand. But initially the early Christians seem to have given no thought to the implications of this; they simply awaited his second coming, which they expected very soon. But with the passage of time, the early Christians naturally reflected on the situation of Jesus between his resurrection and parousia. In the light of this reflection, the idea that Jesus was enthroned at God's right hand at his resurrection developed into the idea that Jesus was exercising rule alongside God in the interval between his resurrection and parousia.[6]

The belief that Jesus presently reigns in heaven is not simply a development of the idea that Jesus was enthroned in heaven at his resurrection. It also rests on the early Christian experience of the present activity of Jesus, especially his sending of the Holy Spirit. Knowing that Jesus was active in their lives before his second coming encouraged them to think of him as presently reigning in heaven. We find one expression of this in Acts 2:33, where Peter interprets the descent of the Holy Spirit at Pentecost by saying that Jesus, "exalted at the right hand of God, and having received from the Father the promise of the Holy Spirit,…has poured out this which you see and hear." Similarly Eph 4:8–11, commenting on Ps 68:18—"he gave gifts to men," says that Jesus "ascended far above all the heavens, that he might fill all things. And his gifts were that some should be apostles, some prophets, some evangelists, some pastors and teachers, etc." These are the gifts of the Spirit.

Another source of the idea that Jesus is presently reigning is interpretation of Old Testament passages, which originally spoke about God, as applying to him. We have already mentioned that expectation of Jesus' second coming partly arose from applying Old Testament passages about the coming of the lord to the coming of the lord Jesus. In the same way, applying Old Testament passages about the reign of the lord to the lord Jesus encouraged the early Christians to see Jesus as presently reigning in heaven. The clearest example of this is found in Phil 2:9–11. In Isa 45:23 God says "To me every knee shall bow, every tongue shall swear." Philippians 2:9–11 says that God has bestowed on Jesus "the name which is above every name, that at the name of Jesus every knee should bow, in heaven and on earth and under the earth, and every tongue confess that Jesus Christ is Lord, to the glory of God the Father." The name which is above every name seems to be 'lord.' It is above every name because it is God's. Giving this name to Jesus implies that he be treated as God is said to be treated in Isa 45:23, i.e., as a king. Thus applying this passage to Jesus has the effect of visualizing Jesus as presently reigning, just as God presently reigns.

The final source of the idea that Jesus is presently reigning is the influence of Hellenistic culture, especially by means of the nuances imparted to the titles lord and Son of God. One indication of this is the acclamation 'Jesus Christ is Lord' which we see in Phil 2:11.[7] Acclamations of the same form were used to acknowledge the divinities of the Hellenistic world. Acknowledging Jesus with the same acclamation would suggest that he is like these divinities. Although this would need qualification, it would support the view that Jesus was presently reigning in heaven. This understanding of Son of God is clear in Rom 1:3–4. Paul refers to Jesus as "descended from David according to the flesh and designated Son of God in power according to the Spirit of holiness by his resurrection from the dead." Son of God had originally been synonymous with Christ and thus with descent from David. Here descent from David is separated from being Son of God, and the latter is said to be "in power," referring to the power of Jesus' present reign.

Although the use of the titles lord and Son of God in the Greek-speaking world strongly encouraged the early Christians to see Jesus as presently reigning in heaven, such an understanding would have been possible even in earliest Palestinian Christianity.[8] Even Aramaic and Hebrew speaking Jews acknowledged the existence of heavenly beings in addition to God, e.g., angels and personified wisdom. Jesus might have been seen as presently reigning with God in heaven by seeing him as one of these. If Jews had not seen any possibility of there being a heavenly being in addition to God, it is doubtful that the early Christians could have embraced this as a way of understanding Jesus. However, it seems that the early Christians began thinking of Jesus as presently reigning in heaven only after the gospel had been proclaimed in Greek. As a matter of fact, Hellenistic culture was an influence on this development.

(b) Expressions of This Belief

In discussing the sources of the belief that Jesus is presently reigning in heaven, we have also seen that this belief was expressed by saying that Jesus had sent the Holy Spirit to his followers after his resurrection, that he was the fulfillment of Old Testament passages like Isa 45:23, and that he had become the Son of God in power at his resurrection. This belief is also expressed in Col 2:15 which says that by his crucifixion Jesus "disarmed the principalities and powers and made a public example of them." This passage expresses the view that Jesus' present reign implies a victory over spiritual powers of evil.

A particularly important expression of the belief that Jesus is presently reigning in heaven involves a new understanding of Ps 110:1. Earlier, as we have seen, this passage was seen as predicting Jesus' second coming when God would make his enemies his footstool. With the development of the belief that Jesus was already reigning in heaven, this passage was reinterpreted as a prediction that at his resurrection Jesus would conquer the powers of evil. We can see this new interpretation of Ps 110:1 in Eph 1:20–23. According to this passage, God raised Jesus from the dead "and made him sit at his right hand in the heavenly places, far above all rule and authority and power and dominion, and above every name that is named,...and he has put all things under his feet..." This passage sees the subjection of all things to Jesus as having occurred already at his resurrection. What has been subjected to him are rule, authority, power and dominion, names for the spiritual powers that dominate the universe.[9]

One thing that allows for this new interpretation of Ps 110:1 is that it is combined with Ps 8:6 which says that God has put all things under the feet of human beings. What is in the future according to Ps 110:1 is past according to Ps 8:6. The latter is explicitly interpreted in Heb 2:5–9. After quoting Ps 110:1 in 1:13, the author quotes Ps 8:4–6 and comments, "Now in putting everything in subjection to him, he left nothing outside his control. As it is, we do not yet see everything in subjection to him. But we see Jesus, who for a little while was made lower than the angels, crowned with glory and honor...." The author acknowledges the hiddenness of the present reign of Jesus, but says that we can affirm this because we have 'seen' the resurrection of Jesus.

A somewhat different interpretation of Ps 110:1 and Ps 8:6 is found in 1 Cor 15:24–25. Here Paul says that at the end Jesus will deliver "the kingdom to God the Father after destroying every rule and every authority and power. For he must reign until he has put all his enemies under his feet." Although it is clear that Paul sees God as the one who ultimately subjects all things to Jesus (cf. vv 27–28), he seems to see Jesus' present reign as a time during which Jesus is in the process of subjecting all spiritual powers to himself. This was not fully accomplished at Jesus' resurrection, but is now in the process of being accomplished.

In Rom 8:34 the belief that Jesus is presently reigning in heaven is expressed by referring to Jesus as being at the right hand of God and interceding for us.

(c) The Belief That Jesus Now Reigns in Heaven in the Letters of Paul

The foregoing discussion of sources and expressions of the belief that Jesus now reigns in heaven has already made it clear that this belief is frequently expressed in the letters of Paul. This belief, though developed in a manner peculiar to Paul, is basic to Paul's explanation of how Jesus did the work of the Christ.[10]

Paul explains how Jesus did the work of the Christ at greatest length in Rom 5:12–6:11. In 5:12–21 Paul argues that Jesus is like Adam. Just as sin and death came into the world through Adam, so grace and life came through Jesus.[11] Paul seems to think of Adam and Jesus as individuals who affect, in opposite ways, the whole human race. The way in which Jesus has this effect is explained in 6:3–11. Christians have been baptized into Jesus (v 3). They are united with him in such a way that they participate in his death and resurrection. In baptism they have already died with Jesus (vv 3–5) and thus died to sin (vv 6–7; cf. vv 10–11). Their participation in the resurrection of Jesus occurs in two stages. In baptism they already enter into newness of life (v 4, 11) and they have the hope of resurrection with Jesus (v 5, 8),[12] presumably at the second coming of Jesus.[13] This idea that believers have died to sin and presently share new life with the risen Jesus is based on the belief that Jesus' death conquered sin and that he presently reigns in heaven. It is Paul's principal explanation of how Jesus did the work of the Christ.

In consequence of this work of Jesus as Christ, those who believe in him form the body of Christ, united with one another by their common unity with Jesus.[14] Paul develops this view of the church at length in Rom 12:3–8 and especially 1 Cor 12:4–30. In the latter passage it is clear that the new life into which one enters in being baptized is the life of the Holy Spirit (v 13). And being baptized into Christ is at the same time being baptized into one body constituted by all those who are baptized. In becoming part of the body of Christ, previously meaningful social distinctions are put aside.[15] They are replaced by the variety of gifts which the Spirit gives (vv 4–11). The church is like a body in consisting of a variety of mutually interdependent members (v 12, 14–26).

Paul's vision of believers as presently sharing new

life with the risen Jesus also comes to expression in many other ways. In 1 Cor 6:12–20 Paul uses the similarity between the relationship created by sexual intercourse and the relationship of Christ and believers (vv 15–17) to argue against patronizing prostitutes. In Eph 5:22–33 (perhaps not written by Paul) this similarity is the basis for exhortation to husbands and wives to behave properly toward each other.

If the account in Acts is reliable at this point, Paul's conversion may have been a significant source of this vision. According to Acts 9:1–5[16] as Paul was on his way to persecute Christians in Damascus, he heard a voice that asked, "Saul, Saul, why do you persecute me?" When Paul asked who was speaking to him, the voice answered, "I am Jesus, whom you are persecuting." This would have told Paul both that Jesus was presently alive and that Jesus identified so fully with the church that to persecute it was to persecute him.

(d) Implications of This Belief

The development of the idea that Jesus presently reigns at the right hand of God is in some ways a simple addition to the expectation that he would come again, making explicit what was implied by the view that his resurrection was his enthronement in heaven. However, it was an idea with important consequences. These can be expressed simply by saying that this belief implied a more exalted understanding of Jesus than did the earlier understanding of how he did the work of the Christ.

Seeing Jesus as the Christ who would come again is to see him in exalted terms. He is the key figure in the most important part of God's plan to save the human race. But even so, he could simply be a human being, one of God's chosen servants, like Moses or the prophets. But seeing him as presently reigning in heaven is to see him as more than human. If he has already conquered the spiritual forces of evil, presently shares in God's rule over the universe, receives universal praise and sends the Holy Spirit, he occupies a status approaching that of God.

This in turn means that Jesus can be prayed to, worshipped. He can become the focus of cultic veneration. Even in the context of expectation of Jesus' parousia, the early Christians prayed *Maranatha*—Our lord, come. But when they saw Jesus as presently reigning in heaven, they could adore him in his present glory and ask for help in meeting present needs. They could act toward him as they acted toward God.

Seeing Jesus as God-like was decisive for the remaining history of faith in Jesus up to the present. Eventually this issued in the doctrine that Jesus was of one substance with the Father, which was defined at the council of Nicea in 325.

Summary

A second explanation of how Jesus did the work of the Christ was the belief that he is presently reigning in heaven. Four factors contributed to the development of this belief:

1. Further reflection on the significance of Jesus' enthronement in heaven at his resurrection;
2. Experience of the present activity of Jesus;
3. Interpretation of Old Testament passages, which originally spoke about God, as applying to Jesus;
4. Influence of Hellenistic culture.

The most important expression of this belief involved a new understanding of Ps 110:1.

This way of understanding how Jesus did the work of the Christ implied a more exalted view of Jesus than did the first explanation.

VII

BELIEF IN THE PREEXISTENCE AND INCARNATION OF JESUS

Partly as a result of the proclamation of the Christian gospel outside of Palestine, the early Christians developed a third explanation of how Jesus did the work of the Christ. As we have seen, the earliest explanation of how Jesus did the work of the Christ was the expectation that he would come again and at that point enter upon his reign. The second explanation of how Jesus did the work of the Christ was the belief that Jesus was already reigning in heaven and thus had secretly begun his reign. The third explanation was based on the belief that Jesus had already been reigning in heaven even before his birth as a human being. With this starting point Jesus does not do the work of the Christ by entering upon his reign, as in the earlier two explanations. Rather, Jesus does the work of the Christ by his incarnation, by becoming human in order to bridge the gulf separating human and divine. His death and resurrection are then primarily his return to where he was before.

Like the belief that Jesus is presently reigning in heaven, belief in his preexistence and incarnation could function as an alternative explanation of how he did the work of the Christ, replacing the earlier two. Some early Christians may have understood Jesus in this way. However, the one New

Testament author who represents this explanation, i.e., the author of the gospel of John, combines it with the other two. Still, the gospel of John puts less emphasis on the expectation that Jesus will come again than do other New Testament writings. This is also true of later Christianity, right up to our own day, which takes a view of Jesus' being the Christ very close to that of John.

Similarly, the understanding of the death and resurrection of Jesus as a return to his starting point with God could be an alternative to seeing it as atonement for sin or victory over the forces of evil. However, in the gospel of John all three views are combined. The death and resurrection of Jesus are seen as atonement, victory and a return to the Father. However, there is less emphasis on the death of Jesus as atoning than in the rest of the New Testament.

1. Sources of This Belief

Before we discuss the factors which gave rise to belief in the preexistence and incarnation of Jesus, we must note that the belief itself seems to precede its use to explain how Jesus is the Christ. Belief in the preexistence and incarnation of Jesus arose within the first twenty years after his death and resurrection; but it was first clearly used to explain how Jesus was the Christ in the gospel of John, written in about 100 CE. Prior to this the preexistence of Jesus was mentioned mainly in order to praise him. The earliest expressions of belief in the preexistence of Jesus are found in material which scholars have identified as hymnic or creedal. Perhaps the early Christians first expressed faith in the preexistence of Jesus as they prayed. When these earliest references are connected with an explanation of how he did the work of the Christ, it is one of the two earlier explanations that we have discussed above.

One source of belief in the preexistence of Jesus may have been reflection on his present exalted status, reigning at the right hand of God. It would certainly be possible to suppose that a human being had been elevated to this status. In the Greco-Roman world the divinization of heroes and emperors would provide analogies to this. But it would also be quite natural to think that someone presently enthroned in heaven must all along have been more than a human being. His present exalted status makes it easy to suppose that Jesus already had such status before his career as a human being.[1]

Another source of the belief in Jesus' preexistence is the interpretation of Old Testament passages, which originally spoke about God, as applying to him. We have already seen that this also entered into development of the expectation of Jesus' second coming and of the idea that he is presently reigning in heaven. In a similar way, applying to Jesus Old Testament passages which spoke about God in the time before Jesus' birth, encouraged the early Christians to see Jesus as having existed before his birth. The clearest example of this is found in John 12:39–41. After quoting Isa 6:10, which is part of the account of Isaiah's inaugural vision of the Lord in the temple, the author of John comments, "Isaiah said this because he saw his glory and spoke of him." John apparently understands Isaiah's vision as a vision of the lord Jesus, who thus existed in the time of Isaiah, approximately 700 years before the birth of Jesus.[2]

A third source of belief in the preexistence of Jesus is the influence of Hellenistic culture, especially by means of the nuances imparted to the titles lord and Son of God (see Chapter VI). One passage which may reflect the influence of a Hellenistic understanding of lord is 1 Cor 8:5–6. After acknowledging the existence of many lords in the Hellenistic world, Paul says that for Christians there is "one Lord, Jesus Christ, through whom are all things and through whom we exist." Though some scholars have argued against this, it seems likely that describing Jesus as the one through whom all things are attributes to him a role in creation, and thus preexistence. Many passages seem to reflect the influence of a Hellenistic understanding of Son of God. Several passages speak of God's sending of his Son.[3] These could presume the preexistence of the Son, though they might also mean simply that Jesus, the Son of God, was sent by God in the same way God sent the prophets. Other passages refer to preexistence more clearly. Hebrews 1:2 says that "in these last days [God] has spoken to us by a Son, whom he appointed the heir of all things, through whom also he created the world." Once again it is the attribution to the Son of a role in creation which implies his preexistence.[4]

A final source of belief in the preexistence of Jesus was the identification of Jesus with the figure of wisdom personified in the Old Testament, and with other comparable figures. The clearest indication of this identification is that Jesus is not only seen as preexistent, but also as having a role in creation. This idea becomes part of the understanding of Jesus as preexistent because Jesus was identified with wisdom which had a role in creation.

2. Wisdom[5]

We first encounter the personification of wisdom in Prov 8:22–31. In this passage wisdom speaks, describing herself as the first creation of God, to whom he gave birth before anything else existed (vv 22–26). She goes on to say that she was with God as he created everything else (vv 27–31) and, comparing herself to a master workman (v 30), suggests that she actively participated in creating. This picture of wisdom is developed at greater length in Wis 6:22–11:1. Here wisdom is described as "a breath of the power of God and a pure emanation of the glory of the Almighty;...a reflection (*apaugasma*) of eternal light, a spotless mirror of the working of God, and an image (*eikon*) of his goodness" (7:25–26). And she is explicitly called the fashioner (*technites*) of all things (7:22). The passage goes on to describe how wisdom preserved the patriarchs, as is narrated in Genesis.

The picture of wisdom was also developed in a somewhat different direction. Wisdom was described as seeking a place to dwell. We find this presentation of wisdom in *1 Enoch* 42:

> Wisdom found no place where she might dwell;
> Then a dwelling-place was assigned her in the heavens.
> Wisdom went forth to make her dwelling among the children
>   of men,
> And found no dwelling place:
> Wisdom returned to her place,
> And took her seat among the angels.[6]

We find this same presentation of wisdom in Sir 24:3–21, but here wisdom takes up her dwelling among the people of Israel, in obedience to the command of God. Thus wisdom was pictured as a being who was with God from the beginning and participated in the creation of the world. She could also be pictured as leaving her heavenly dwelling place to seek a dwelling among humans, and then returning to heaven.[7]

Of course, there is no serious possibility that Jesus either resembled the figure of wisdom, or claimed to be that figure.[8] But the early Christians connected Jesus with wisdom in at least two ways. First, the salvation accomplished by God through the death and resurrection of Jesus was understood as the preeminent manifestation of divine wisdom. And second, the words and deeds of Jesus were understood as indicating that he was an emissary of wisdom, or even wisdom herself.

We see the first of these connections reflected in the only New Testament passage in which Jesus is explicitly said to be wisdom, i.e., 1 Cor 1:24 where Paul says that Christ is the wisdom of God. The second of these connections is strongly implied in Matt 11:2–19. At the beginning of the passage the author says that John the Baptist had heard about the deeds of the Christ, i.e., the miracles of Jesus described in chapters 8–9. The passage ends with Jesus' responding to his critics by saying, "Wisdom is justified by her deeds." Matthew seems to be implying that the deeds of Christ are also the deeds of wisdom. We can see that Matthew did identify Jesus with wisdom by considering Matt 23:34. Here Matthew attributes to Jesus a saying which was probably attributed to wisdom by Q.[9] This shows us that Matthew thought of Jesus as wisdom, though this would not have been apparent to his readers.[10]

In none of these passages is it clear that the identification of Jesus with wisdom implies his preexistence. However, eventually Jesus was identified with preexistent wisdom. This identification is most clearly found where Jesus is described in terms synonymous with wisdom, but where the term 'wisdom' itself is not used.

In Col 1:15–16 Jesus is described as "the image of the invisible God, the first-born of all creation; for in him all things were created." Though some have argued the contrary,[11] this seems to present Jesus as preexistent and as having had a role in creation.[12] Though the term wisdom is not used, an identification with wisdom seems to underlie this. As we have seen, wisdom is called the image of God in Wis 7:26. And wisdom is seen as having been brought forth by God and as having participated in creation in Prov 8:22–31 and elsewhere. Wisdom is called the image of

God by means of an interpretation of Gen 1:26–27 which speaks of creation of human beings in the image of God.[13]

Hebrews 1:2–3 refers to Jesus as the son of God, "through whom...he created the world. He reflects the glory of God and bears the very stamp of his nature, upholding the universe by his word of power." Again an identification with wisdom seems to underlie this passage even though the term wisdom is not used. Wisdom is called the reflection (*apaugasma*) of eternal light in Wis 7:26; *apaugasma* is the word translated "he reflects" in Heb 1:3. And once again there is reference to wisdom as the offspring of God who participated in creation.

Finally John 1:1–18 refers to Jesus as the word who was with God in the beginning (v 1), through whom all things were made (vv 3, 10), who came into the world and dwelt among humans (vv 9–14). An identification with wisdom underlies this passage, though Jesus is called word rather than wisdom. In a passage like Wis 9:1–2 we can see word used as a parallel to wisdom. God is addressed as the one "who has made all things by your word, and by your wisdom has formed man." However, John's use of word for Jesus in 1:1–18 probably rests on Old Testament and Hellenistic Jewish talk about the word of God, not simply on the equivalence of word and wisdom. Still it seems clear that the figure of wisdom underlies John 1:1–18. Like wisdom, the word exists prior to creation, is the agent of creation, and seeks a dwelling among humans.

3. Expressions of Belief in the Preexistence and Incarnation of Jesus

In discussing the sources of belief in Jesus' preexistence, we have also seen that this belief was expressed by

saying that Jesus was the referent of Old Testament passages like Isa 6:10, by calling him the lord or Son of God
through whom all was created, and by identifying him
with the figure of wisdom, using a variety of terms—
image, reflection, word of God.[14] This belief is also
expressed in other ways.

The earliest expression of belief in the preexistence
and incarnation of Jesus is probably Phil 2:6–11. This passage is probably an early hymn or creed which Paul
quotes in his letter to the Philippians. It describes the
career of Jesus as beginning in the exalted state of being in
the form (*morphe*) of God and equal (*isa*) to God (v 6). Then
Jesus emptied himself, having taken the form of a slave,
being in the likeness of human beings (v 7). He then hum-
bled himself and suffered crucifixion (v 8). Therefore God
exalted him, making him the object of universal acclaim
(vv 9–11). This seems to be a complete statement of belief
in the preexistence of Jesus. Jesus began as a heavenly
being; he emptied himself, entering into the human
sphere; and in his death and resurrection he returned to
his beginning point. The only thing missing is that Jesus'
entry into the human world is not said to have any salvific
significance. The hymn may simply praise Jesus for his
remarkable career. Paul cites it as an example of the attitude which should characterize the Philippians.

In recent years there has been considerable discussion
about the meaning of saying that Jesus was in the form of
God and equal to God. Attempting to avoid imposing
later beliefs on the text, some have argued that being in
the form of God and equal to God indicates not the preexistence of Jesus, but rather his being in the pre-lapsarian
state of Adam.[15] Being in the form of God means being in
the image of God in which Adam was first created. Not
regarding equality with God something to be grasped
means avoiding the temptation to which Adam suc-

cumbed, to become like God by eating the forbidden fruit. This is certainly plausible. However, with the majority of scholars I am still inclined to see Phil 2:6–11 as an expression of belief in Jesus' preexistence. Even if the underlying thought is a comparison between Jesus and Adam, it still seems most likely that Jesus is understood to begin in a preexistent state.

A second expression of belief in the preexistence of Jesus may be found in 2 Cor 8:9—"For you know the grace of our Lord Jesus Christ, that though he was rich, yet for your sake he became poor, so that by his poverty you might become rich." Paul says this as he tries to persuade the Corinthians to contribute to the collection he is taking up. This may account for his use of the terms rich and poor. What rich and poor mean in relation to Jesus Paul does not explain. In the light of Phil 2:6–11 it seems likely that he is referring to the preexistent state of Jesus as being rich, and to his emptying himself and becoming a man as being poor. Just as there is doubt that this is the meaning of the Philippians passage, there is even more doubt that this is the meaning of this passage.[16] The meaning of the passage cannot be established with certainty. However, along with most scholars, I am inclined to see it as a reference to the preexistence of Jesus.

A third passage which may express belief in the preexistence of Jesus is Eph 4:8–10. Commenting on Ps 68:19, which refers to someone ascending on high, the passage says, "In saying, 'He ascended,' what does it mean but that he had also descended into the lower parts of the earth? He who descended is he who also ascended far above all the heavens, that he might fill all things." It is debated whether descent into the lower parts of the earth means descent from heaven into the human world, i.e., implies preexistence, or means descent into Hades, the place of the dead.[17]

Finally, the letter to the Hebrews speaks of Jesus as preexistent at other points in addition to Heb 1:2–3. The clearest passage is 10:5–7. Here Ps 40:6–8 is interpreted as something said by Christ when he came into the world. Likewise, in 2:9, Ps 8:4–6 is interpreted as applying to Jesus. In saying that Jesus "for a little while was made lower than the angels," the author may be thinking that in his preexistent state Jesus was superior to the angels.[18]

4. The Preexistence and Incarnation of Jesus in the Gospel of John

As we have already noted, the only New Testament writing which explains how Jesus did the work of the Christ in terms of preexistence and incarnation is the gospel of John. We have also seen that John expresses the preexistence and incarnation of Jesus in 12:39–41, where Isa 6:10 is understood as referring to the preexistent Jesus, and in 1:1–18, where Jesus is interpreted in terms of the figure of wisdom. The preexistence and incarnation of Jesus is also expressed in many other ways in the gospel of John. For example, in 17:5, 24, Jesus says that he shared glory with the Father before the world was made. In 8:56–58 Jesus says that he existed before the time of Abraham. John refers to Jesus as the Son of man who has descended from heaven,[19] as the light that has come into the world,[20] and as having come from above,[21] or from heaven,[22] or from God.[23] Most commonly of all John refers to Jesus as having been sent by God.[24]

For John the incarnation of the eternal Word of God in Jesus (1:14) is salvific because it alone makes God accessible to human beings. Three times John says that no one has ever seen God,[25] indicating the limit on human access to God. But such access to God is necessary for human beings to have life, in the fullest sense. Therefore, God sent the Word into the world, incarnate in Jesus, in order to make God known. As it says in 1:18, "No one has ever seen God; the only Son, who is in the bosom of the Father, he has made him known."

The central message of the gospel of John is that Jesus was sent by the Father to make the Father known. John uses various images to present Jesus as the one who reveals the Father. Saying that Jesus is the incarnation (1:14) of the Word that was with God from the beginning (1:1) in itself implies the revelatory character of Jesus; just as our words reveal us, so the eternal word reveals God. John also presents Jesus as the revealer of the Father by speaking of him as the witness of the Father,[26] the messenger of the Father,[27] the Son who does what he sees his Father doing,[28] etc. Jesus' revelatory character is stated most directly in 14:8–11. In response to Philip's request that Jesus show the Father to his disciples, Jesus says, "He who has seen me has seen the Father" (v 9).

Simply by being the Word made flesh Jesus makes God accessible and so performs the work of the Christ. However, as John makes clear, Jesus was not obviously the Word made flesh. Jesus' claim to be the incarnate Word was rejected by many.[29] But those who did believe that he was the incarnate Word thereby gained access to God and thus eternal life. Faith in Jesus confers eternal life.[30]

Jesus' death and resurrection is primarily his return to the Father, the restoration of the glory he had before the incarnation.[31] But this return to the Father is also the foundation for faith. It is when one sees Jesus' return to the Father that one can most readily believe that he came from the Father to make the Father known. Three times in the gospel of John Jesus predicts that the Son of man will be lifted up so that all may believe in him and so have eternal life.[32] This lifting up includes Jesus' death, resurrection and return to the Father.

5. Implications of This Belief

We have already seen that development of the belief that Jesus is presently reigning in heaven implied an exalted understanding of Jesus according to which he occupied a status approaching that of God. Development of belief in his preexistence made him even more like God. Conceiving of Jesus in increasingly God-like terms made it necessary to explain how this could be. The early Christians could not, like their non-Christian Gentile contemporaries, simply accept the existence of more than one God. Nor could they replace God with Jesus. In the New Testament writings we find no explanation of how Jesus can be so like God, yet distinct from God. The two are simply asserted.

Thus in Phil 2:6–11 Jesus is said to have begun in the form of God and equal to God, and to end with the name that is above every name, receiving universal acclaim. But it is God who exalts Jesus and bestows the name on him, and the acclaim given Jesus is to the glory of God. In Col 1:15–20 Jesus is said to be the image of God in whom the fullness of God dwelt. But it is God who, through Jesus, reconciles all things to himself. In Heb 1:1–4 Jesus is said to reflect the glory of God, bear the stamp of his nature and uphold the universe by his word. But after making purification for sins Jesus sat down at the right hand of God. And in John 1:1 it says both that the Word was God and that the Word was with God.

In the way that I have tried to describe, the early Christians were led to a view of Jesus as God-like before they could explain how this was compatible with their belief that there was only one God, and that God was distinct from Jesus. In later centuries they sorted this out by means of the doctrine of the Trinity, which provided a way to say that Jesus was divine, despite the fact that there was only one God and that God was distinct from Jesus. According to this doctrine there is one divine substance, but three divine persons. Thus Jesus and God are one substance, but distinct persons.

Summary

A third explanation of how Jesus did the work of the Christ was provided by the belief that he had existed before his birth as a human being. Four factors contributed to the development of this belief:

1. Further reflection on the present exalted status of Jesus;
2. Interpretation of Old Testament passages, which originally spoke about God, as applying to Jesus;
3. Influence of Hellenistic culture;
4. Identification of Jesus with wisdom.

This belief is most often expressed in hymns or creeds, but is also found elsewhere. In the New Testament it is used to explain how Jesus did the work of the Christ in the gospel of John.

This way of understanding how Jesus did the work of the Christ implied an even more exalted view of Jesus than did the second explanation, giving him a status approaching that of God.

USE OF TITLES FOR JESUS IN THE EARLY DEVELOPMENT OF CHRISTIAN FAITH

During the Life of Jesus	After the Death and Resurrection of Jesus and the Origin of Belief that He is the Christ		
	Three explanations of how Jesus did the work of the Christ *Increasing influence of Hellenistic culture*		
	Expectation that Jesus will come again	**Belief that Jesus now reigns in heaven**	**Belief in the preexistence and incarnation of Jesus**
Son of man Lord Son of God	Son of man Lord Son of God	Lord Son of God	Lord Son of God Wisdom (image, word)
	Jesus' Life, Death and Resurrection as Atonement	**Jesus' Life, Death and Resurrection as Victory**	**Jesus' Death and Resurrection as Return**
Prophet	Suffering servant Prophet Son of God Priest		

VIII.

CONCLUSION

1. Summary

In the preceding pages I have outlined the way in which the early Christians came to believe that Jesus was the Christ, and the development of that belief in the next twenty years, a development partly required by the starting point.

We have seen that Jesus did not greatly resemble the expected Christ, and did not make any emphatic claim to be the Christ. Nevertheless, the early Christians recognized him as the Christ. He had been crucified as a pretender to the title of Christ, but God had raised him from the dead, implicitly reversing the judgment that Jesus was not the Christ and declaring him to be the Christ. The resurrection, in the context of Jesus' crucifixion as false Christ, was the foundation for the belief that Jesus was the Christ.

The early Christians supported this belief in two ways. First, they supported the claim that Jesus was the Christ by showing that he was the fulfillment of scripture. The Christ was expected as the fulfillment of scriptural promises. Prior to the recognition of Jesus as the Christ, scripture had been read as promising a very different sort of Christ than Jesus. But when the early Christians read scripture with the assurance that Jesus was the Christ, they were able to find many scriptural predictions of precisely the kind of Christ he was. This reading of scripture was so successful that many Christians today are unaware of its dependence on faith in Jesus as the Christ.

Second, the early Christians supported their belief in Jesus as the Christ by explaining how he did the work of the Christ. The earliest and most fundamental explanation was that Jesus would come again and would then do all that the Christ had been expected to do. This explanation conserved all of the pre-Christian expectation of the Christ by assigning it to a second coming of the Christ. But this acutely raised the question of the meaning of the Christ's first coming. The earliest and most fundamental answer to this question was that the death of Jesus was an atonement for sin.

Somewhat later the early Christians developed a second and third explanation of how Jesus did the work of the Christ. Both of these resulted from working out the implications of their faith in Jesus, but also from the influence of Hellenistic culture as the gospel was proclaimed and believed outside of Palestine.

The second explanation of how Jesus did the work of the Christ was that Jesus was already reigning in heaven. Not only would he return to establish the kingdom of God; he had already established it in a hidden way and was presently ruling over it from heaven. When Jesus was seen as doing the work of the Christ in this way, his life, death and resurrection became the means by which he overcame the forces of evil and established God's kingdom.

The third explanation of how Jesus did the work of the Christ was belief in the preexistence and incarnation of Jesus. Not only would he return to establish the kingdom of God; not only had he already established it in a hidden way immediately after his resurrection; he had already established it even before his birth as a human being. When Jesus was seen in this way, he was understood to do the work of the Christ by his incarnation, becoming human in order to reunite the divine and human realms. His death and resurrection were his return to where he was before. Belief in the preexistence and incarnation of Jesus developed within the first twenty years after his death and resurrection, but this belief was not clearly used to explain how Jesus did the work of the Christ until approximately 100 CE when the gospel of John was written.

With this third explanation of how Jesus did the work of the Christ, we come very close to the understanding of this which we take for granted today. This explanation absorbs the second very completely. Just as Jesus was enthroned in heaven before his birth as a human being, so he has resumed that station since his death and resurrection. The first explanation is not taken up so completely. The work of the Christ has been so fully accomplished by his life, death and resurrection that there seems slight need for a second coming of the Christ. However, this can still be awaited as the time when what is already true will become manifest.

2. Implications

This account of the origin and development of Christian faith has several implications on which I will comment briefly. First, the death and resurrection of Jesus are more important than the life of Jesus for the development of Christian faith. I do not mean to set the life of Jesus completely over against his death and resurrection. I have tried to show that there is considerable continuity between the life of Jesus and the faith of his followers after his death and resurrection. But what the early Christians believed about Jesus was essentially that he had died and risen and so was the Christ, not that he had taught certain things or lived in a certain way. This must be emphasized because the existence of the gospels, and thus of extensive presentations of the life and teachings of Jesus, permits and even encourages people to suppose that this is what is most significant about Jesus. From some perspectives it may be what is most important, but not if we are concerned with Christian faith. The faith of the church is primarily concerned with the death and resurrection of Jesus and its implications, and only secondarily with the life and teachings of Jesus. This is true in a sense even from the perspective of belief in the preexistence of Jesus. From this point of view it is the fact of the incarnation, not the details of Jesus' life and teaching, which is crucial.

Second, if the death and resurrection of Jesus are the starting point for Christian faith in the way I have outlined, this sets limits on possible understandings of the resurrection.[1] The resurrection must have been something capable of reversing the meaning of Jesus' crucifixion. Jesus was crucified as a false Christ, and crucifying Jesus would itself have validated that verdict. It seems impossible that someone who had simply been crucified could have been acknowledged as the Christ. It was the resurrection that allowed for this possibility. Therefore the resurrection must have been something that could produce this effect. It is easiest to suppose that the New Testament is reliable at this point and that what happened was that certain people saw Jesus after his death, and perhaps saw his empty tomb. But whatever happened, it must have been something that could give an entirely new meaning to Jesus' death. It is necessary to emphasize this because the resurrection has been discussed extensively in recent years. Much of the discussion attempts to reconcile the miraculous character of the resurrection with our skepticism about miracles, by explaining it reductionistically as a psychological phenomenon. However, in order for the resurrection to have had the effect it had on the development of Christian faith, it must have had a certain measure of objective unexpectedness. This is sometimes neglected in discussion of the resurrection that construes its impact on the emergence of Christian faith differently than I have.[2]

Third, if Christian faith developed in the way I have outlined, it is clear that belief in Jesus is precisely a matter of faith. It is not possible to prove that Jesus is the Christ, only to believe it. It is possible to show that this belief is reasonable in various ways—that it is not absurd to accept the word of those who said they had seen Jesus risen, that Jesus can be seen as the fulfillment of scripture, that the development of Christian faith is coherent. However, it is only possible to acknowledge Jesus as the Christ by believing it, and this entails various kinds of faith. It entails faith that those Jewish people who expected the coming of the Christ were guided by the Holy Spirit into a true interpretation of their scriptures and tradition, even though, as we have seen, this had not always been part of Judaism. It entails faith that those who claimed Jesus had been raised by God were telling the truth. And it entails faith that the early Christians who expected Jesus to come again, saw him as presently reigning in heaven and thought that he had existed before his birth as a human being, were guided by the Holy Spirit into a true understanding of the meaning of Jesus' being the Christ. Recognizing the primacy of faith can be important in Jewish-Christian dialogue. We can understand that not all Jews still look for the coming of the Christ. And we can understand that those who do, could never recognize Jesus as the Christ without faith in his resurrection. Further, we can easily see why so many Jews did not recognize Jesus as the Christ in the past. This is not surprising. What is surprising is that so many Jews did accept Jesus as the Christ.

Finally, this account of the origins of Christian faith may allow us to distinguish between more fundamental and less fundamental Christian beliefs.[3] Of course, the entire development is reflected in the New Testament which means that all elements of it are normative for Christian theology. However, there seems to be the possibility of some discriminations even within that. What seems most fundamental of all is that Jesus was crucified, raised from the dead, and is the Christ. This is the irreducible core of Christian faith. If we arrange the other elements of Christian faith chronologically, next in importance is the belief that as Christ Jesus fulfilled the Old Testament. Next is the belief that he will do the work of the Christ when he comes again. Last in importance are the beliefs that he presently reigns in heaven and that he existed before his birth as a human being. Instead of chronologically, we could also arrange these in an order of theological profundity. This would simply reverse the order above, making the last chronologically first theologically. This is the approach implicit in Christian theology in general. However, at one time Christians probably did believe in Jesus as the Christ without the final stage or the one before that. This seems to open up the possibility of different kinds of authentic Christian faith than the one most familiar to us. This could be important in the dialogue between Christianity and other religions.

For example, one problem which Christian faith presents for Jews is the doctrine of the Trinity, particularly the belief that Jesus was divine as well as human. Since there was a time when Christians believed in Jesus as the Christ without believing that he was divine, might such a view of Jesus still be a possibility for Jews today? Historically the Christian church has said not. Is there any possibility of giving a different answer now?

NOTES

I. Introduction

[1]If we suppose that certain beliefs about Jesus which are not mentioned in 1 Thessalonians did not come into being before they were mentioned in other letters of Paul, we might need to extend this period by about five years. On the other hand, if we suppose that the faith which Paul expresses in his letters was already known to him at the time of his conversion, we could reduce this period by fifteen years or more; Paul probably became a follower of Jesus only a few years after the death and resurrection of Jesus. In any case this development occurred within a surprisingly short time.

[2]On this see Brown, "Who Do Men Say That I Am?"

[3]So also Bultmann, *Theology of the New Testament*, 1.43; Dahl, "The Crucified Messiah," *Jesus the Christ*, 27–47; Fredriksen, *From Jesus to Christ*, 136. Jonge (*Christology in Context*, 208–11) acknowledges the centrality of the confession, but does not go so far as to say it was the starting point of Christian faith.

[4]On this see Horsley, "Popular Messianic Movements."

[5]See also Matt 2:4; Mark 12:35–37/Matt 22:41–46/Luke

20:41–44; Luke 3:15; John 7:27, 31, 41–42; 12:34 and Acts 2:31.

[6]On this see Dahl, "The Messiahship of Jesus in Paul," *Jesus the Christ*, 15–25; Hengel, "'Christos' in Paul," *Between Jesus and Paul*, 65–77.

[7]However, the gospels, Acts, Revelation and 1 and 2 John also use 'Christ' in ways that show awareness of its original meaning and connotations. In Revelation and Luke-Acts 'Christ' is used with a genitive, e.g., "our Lord and…his Christ" (Rev 11:15), Jesus as "the Christ of God" (Luke 9:20). In the gospels and Acts we find discussions concerning the doctrinal concept of the Christ (e.g., Mark 12:35–37 and parallels; John 7:40–42). In these writings and 1 and 2 John 'Christ' is predicated of Jesus (e.g., 1 John 2:22). In different ways these writings reflect a Jewish context in which the term 'Christ' is understood.

[8]Cf. Acts 11:26.

II. Recognition of Jesus As the Christ: The Problem

[1]See surveys of this in Cullmann, *Christology*, 113–17; Hahn, *Titles*, 136–48; Fuller, *Foundations*, 23–31; Jonge, "The Use of the Word 'Anointed;'" "The Earliest Christian Use of Christos"; Grundmann *et al.*, "*chriō ktl.*," 496–527; Vermes, *Jesus the Jew*, 129–59; Leivestad, *Jesus*, 48–63.

[2]Other statements of this promise are found in Pss 89:3–4, 28–37; 132:11–12.

[3]This hope is reflected in passages like Isa 9:6–7; 11.

[4]Such an expectation seems to be reflected in Jer 30:8–9

and Ezek 37:21–25, both coming from shortly after the Babylonian conquest.

⁵The translation is adapted from that of Charles, *Apocrypha and Pseudepigrapha* 2.649–50. The translation of line 27 (= *Pss. Sol.* 17:32) is based on emendation of the text. All manuscripts agree that the line should read, "For all shall be holy, and their king the Lord Christ" [my translation]. On this see Charlesworth, *Old Testament Pseudepigrapha* 2.667–68 note z. Other references to the Christ are found in *Pss. Sol.* 18, title and vv 5 and 7.

⁶1QS 9.11; CD 12.23–13.1, 14.19, 19.10–11, 20.1; 4QPatr; 4Q252; 4Q521.

⁷My translation of the text found in Lohse, *Die Texte aus Qumran*, 50.

⁸My translation of the text in Lohse, *Die Texte aus Qumran*, 58–60. Other references to the Christ are found in *1 Enoch* 48:10 and 52:4; the date of these passages is uncertain. We also find references to the Christ in *4 Ezra* 12:32 and *2 Apoc. Bar.* 29:3; 30:1; 39:7; 40:1; 70:9; 72:2, dating from the end of the first century CE.

⁹See lines 11–17, 21.

¹⁰Psalms of Solomon, line 1; Eschatological Rule, lines 2-3; Blessings, line 12.

¹¹Psalms of Solomon, lines 5, 18, 25, 35, 38–41; Blessings, lines 5, 10.

¹²Psalms of Solomon, lines 1–2; Blessings, lines 2–3.

[13]Psalms of Solomon, lines 12, 18; Blessings, lines 3–5.

[14]Blessings, lines 6–7.

[15]Psalms of Solomon, lines 3–10; Blessings, lines 9, 11.

[16]Blessings, lines 3–5.

[17]Psalms of Solomon, lines 19, 32; Blessings, line 12.

[18]Psalms of Solomon, lines 22–27.

[19]Psalms of Solomon, lines 8, 33 = Blessings, line 9; Psalms of Solomon, lines 38–39 = Blessings, line 10.

[20]Jonge (*Christology in Context*, 167, 211) argues that since David is portrayed as prophet and exorcist, these activities on Jesus' part would increase his resemblance to the expected Davidic Christ.

[21]Mark 14:61–62; John 4:25–26; 17:3.

[22]Luke 23:2 (cf. John 19:12).

[23]Mark 9:41; Mark 12:35–37/Matt 22:41–46/Luke 20:41–44; Mark 13:21/Matt 24:23; Matt 23:10; Matt 24:5.

[24]Mark 8:27–33/Matt 16:13–23/Luke 9:18–22; Mark 15:2–5/Matt 27:11–14/Luke 23:2–5 (cf. John 18:33–38); Matt 26:63–64/Luke 22:67–70; Luke 23:39–43; John 10:24–25.

[25]Mark 11:1–10/Matt 21:1–9/Luke 19:28–38/John 12:12–15.

[26]Matt 26:63–64/Luke 22:67–70.

[27]On this see Bultmann, *Theology of the New Testament*, 1.27; Cullmann, *Christology*, 117–26; Hahn, *Titles*, 148–61; Fuller, *Foundations*, 109–11; Conzelmann, *Outline of Theology*, 129–30. For recent arguments that Jesus did claim to be the Christ see Chapter III, nn 1 and 9 below.

[28]Note that both Matthew and Luke have told this story in a way suggesting that Peter's understanding of Jesus is adequate. In Matthew Jesus responds to Peter's identification of him as the Christ by saying, "Blessed are you, Simon Bar-Jona! For flesh and blood has not revealed this to you, but my Father who is in heaven" (16:17). Luke omits Peter's rebuke of Jesus and Jesus' rebuke of Peter. These versions of the story probably show more influence of Christian faith than does Mark's.

[29]This verse is explicitly quoted by Matthew (21:5) and John (12:15).

III. Recognition of Jesus as the Christ: A Solution

[1]See "The Crucified Messiah," *Jesus the Christ*, 27–47. Others who have perceived the problem have offered other solutions. Cullmann (*Christology*, 134), followed by Fuller (*Foundations*, 159), argues that only by using the title 'Christ' were the disciples "able to make their faith in Jesus understandable to the Jews of their time." Hahn (*Titles*, 148) criticizes this view; he himself considers the use of the title a relatively late development which occurred when the idea of the Christ, modified by "the influence of apocalyptic thought," was applied to the second coming of Jesus (ibid., 162). Berger ("Die königlichen Messiastraditionen," 1–2) rejects Hahn's view and argues that the basic meaning of calling Jesus 'Christ' was not to

identify him with the eschatological king expected by Israel, but rather to designate him as a prophetic bearer of teaching and revelation. Sanders (*Jesus and Judaism*, 228–34), followed by Fredriksen (*From Jesus to Christ*, 141), argues that Jesus' disciples called him Christ because he was their leader and claimed exceptional personal authority as forerunner of the kingdom. Harvey (*Jesus and the Constraints*, 136–42) argues that Jesus' disciples called him the Christ after his resurrection because Jesus had already been called the Christ before his resurrection, meaning that Jesus was the one anointed with the spirit described in Isa 61:1.

[2]Mark 15:26/Matt 27:37/Luke 23:38/John 19:19.

[3]Mark 15:2 and parallels, including John 18:33–38.

[4]Mark 15:9 and parallels; 15:12; John 19:12–15.

[5]Mark 15:16–20 and parallels.

[6]Mark 15:32. Matt 27:42 has "the King of Israel"; Luke 23:35 has "the Christ of God, his Chosen One." According to Matt 2:1–4, the magi came to Jerusalem seeking the one born king of the Jews, and Herod responded by asking the chief priests and scribes where the Christ was to be born.

[7]Cf. Mark 15:2 and parallels.

[8]"The Crucified Messiah," 43.

[9]Van Unnik ("Jesus the Christ") accepts Dahl's explanation, but adds to it that Jesus was recognized as the Christ during his lifetime on the basis of his anointing by the Spirit of God. And for this reason he was put to death.

Betz (*What Do We Know About Jesus?*, 86), Marshall (*Origins*, 61 n 37, 90, 93–94), Moule (*Origin of Christology*, 31–35), Leivestad (*Jesus*, 95–96), and Jonge (*Christology in Context*, 209–11) reject Dahl's explanation and derive early Christian use of Christ for Jesus from Jesus' own use of it for himself. Casey likewise rejects Dahl's view (*From Jewish Prophet*, 43–44) and derives early Christian use of Christ for Jesus from "Jesus' position as the central identity factor of the Christian community" (ibid., 105).

[10]On this see Dahl, "Eschatology and History in Light of the Qumran Texts," *Jesus the Christ*, 49–64.

[11]On this see G. Scholem, "Sabbatianism and Mystical Heresy."

[12]For general discussion of this topic see Dodd, *According to the Scriptures*; Lindars, *New Testament Apologetic*; Juel, *Messianic Exegesis*.

[13]See for example, Dahl, "The Atonement: An Adequate Reward for the Akedah?" *Jesus the Christ*, 137–51. In addition to making reference to the ways in which Jesus fulfilled the Hebrew scriptures, the early Christians made other kinds of reference to the scriptures. These can be summarized under three headings. 1. The early Christians made frequent reference to the laws of the Hebrew scriptures, considering whether, or in what way, these constituted ethical guidelines for them. 2. Occasionally the early Christians discussed the theology of the Hebrew scriptures in order to argue that following Jesus was in accord with them. We find this particularly in Galatians, Romans and Hebrews. 3. Occasionally the early Christians spoke about promises of the Hebrew scriptures as still to be fulfilled in the future.

[14]Cf. Rom 1:2–4.

[15]Cf. similar statements in Luke 24:26–27; 44–46; Acts 17:2–3. Acts 3:18 and 13:27–29 refer to prophetic prediction of the suffering of the Christ.

[16]Mark 8:31 and parallels.

[17]Tödt (*Son of Man,* 162, 165) argues that Ps 118:22 underlies Mark 8:31; 9:12.

[18]We find an allusion to the passage in this sense in Acts 4:10–11.

[19]In the same place Jesus is also seen as fulfilling two other passages that mention a stone—Isa 28:16 (1 Pet 2:6) and Isa 8:14–15 (1 Pet 2:8).

[20]Mark 12:10–11 and parallels.

[21]Mark 14:34/Matt 26:38.

[22]On this see Hay, *Glory at the Right Hand;* Gourgues, *A la Droite de Dieu;* Hengel, "Ps 110 und die Erhöhung des Auferstandenen."

[23]In Eph 1:22 Ps 8:6 is also seen as having been fulfilled by Jesus' resurrection. In 1 Cor 15:27 the fulfillment of Ps 8:6 is understood to lie in the future.

[24]Heb 1:3; 8:1; 10:12.

[25]Mark 14:62/Matt 26:64/Luke 22:69.

[26]This passage is explicitly quoted in Mark 12:36 and parallels. Cf. also Mark 16:19.

[27]Cf. also Mark 8:31; 9:31; 10:34 and parallels; Luke 24:46; Acts 10:40.

[28]Matthew omits Mark 8:18; Luke omits Mark 7:6–7 and 8:18.

[29]Matthew's other 'formula quotations' are found in 2:6, 15, 18, 23; 4:15–16; 8:17; 12:18–21; 13:35; 21:5; 27:9–10.

[30]Ps 18:49; Deut 32:43; Ps 117:1 and Isa 11:10.

[31]Cf. Luke 2:32.

[32]Isa 10:22–23; 1:9; and 28:16.

[33]Note that in Rom 11:26–27 Paul argues that the ultimate salvation of all Israel will fulfill Isa 59:20–21. This belongs to the category of scriptural promises whose fulfillment still lies in the future, but is worth noting alongside the view that Israel's unbelief fulfills scripture.

[34]On expression of the expectation that Jesus will come again in the gospels, see Chapter IV. On the interpretation of Jesus' death as atonement in the gospels, see Chapter V. On the understanding of Jesus as presently reigning in heaven in Luke-Acts, see Chapter VI. And on the understanding of Jesus as preexistent in John, see Chapter VII.

[35]Luke 18:31–33; 24:26–27, 44–46; Acts 17:2–3; cf. 3:18; 13:27–29.

[36]Luke 20:17; Acts 4:10–11.

[37]Luke 22:69; Acts 2:34–36.

[38]Acts 2:25–31; 13:35.

[39]Acts 3:22–23.

[40]Acts 13:33–34.

[41]Dahl, "The Purpose of Luke-Acts," 89.

[42]Cf. also Luke 24:26–27, 44–46; Acts 2:30–32; 3:18; 13:27–33.

[43]For a discussion of the views that Luke-Acts distorts the kerygma and has replaced a theology of the cross with a theology of glory see Fitzmyer, *Gospel According to Luke,* 11–14, 22–23. Fitzmyer himself argues against these views.

[44]Most scholars regard Luke-Acts as addressed to Gentiles; for this view see Fitzmyer, *Gospel According to Luke,* 57–59. However, recently some have argued, correctly I believe, that Luke-Acts addresses the concerns of Jewish Christians. These include Jervell, *Luke and the People of God* and Esler, *Community and Gospel.* See also Callan, "Background of the Apostolic Decree."

[45]E.g., the letter of Barnabas and especially Justin's *Dialogue with Trypho.*

IV. The Expectation That Jesus Will Come Again

[1]We find explicit argument along these lines in Justin's *Dialogue with Trypho.* For example, in 31–32 Justin says that Dan 7:9–28 refers to the second coming of Jesus, while Isa 52:13–53:12 refers to his first coming. Justin also refers to

scriptural predictions of the two comings of Jesus in 14; 52–53 and 110–11.

[2]See the surveys of this title in Cullmann, *Christology,* 137–92; Tödt, *Son of Man;* Hahn, *Titles,* 15–67; Fuller, *Foundations,* 34–43; Vermes, *Jesus the Jew,* 160–91; Marshall, *Origins,* 63–82; Fitzmyer, "The NT Title 'Son of Man'"; Dunn, *Christology,* 65–97; Leivestad, *Jesus,* 153–68; Hare, *Son of Man Tradition.*

[3]Heb 2:6 quotes Ps 8:5, and Rev 1:13; 14:14 allude to Dan 7:13.

[4]E.g., Cullmann, *Christology,* 137–42; Hahn, *Titles,* 17; Fuller, *Foundations,* 34–43.

[5]E.g., Perrin, "Apocalyptic Son of Man Sayings"; Casey, *Son of Man,* 99–141; Dunn, *Christology,* 67–82; Lindars, *Jesus Son of Man,* 1–16; Jonge, *Christology in Context,* 171; Hare, *Son of Man Tradition,* 235–44.

[6]E.g., 1QS 11.20; 1QH 4.30.

[7]Son of man sayings are found in the following passages:

Mark 2:10/Matt 9:6/Luke 5:24	Matt 8:20/Luke 9:58
28/Matt 12:8/Luke 6:5	10:23
8:31/Luke 9:22	11:19/Luke 7:34
38/Matt 16:27/Luke 9:26	12:32/Luke 12:10
9:9/Matt 17:9	40/Luke 11:30
12/Matt 17:12	13:37
31/Matt 17:22/Luke 9:44	41
10:33–4/Matt 20:18–19/Luke 18:31–33	16:13
45/Matt 20:28	27–28
13:26/Matt 24:30/Luke 21:27	(18:11)
14:21/Matt 26:24/Luke 22:22	19:28

Mark 14:41/Matt 26:45	Matt 24:27/Luke 17:24
62/Matt 26:64/Luke 22:69	37/Luke 17:26
	39/Luke 17:30
	44/Luke 12:40
	25:31
	26:2

Luke 6:22	John 1:51
(9:56)	3:13
12:8	14
17:22	5:27
18:8	6:27
19:10	53
21:36	62
22:48	8:28
24:7	9:35
	12:23
	34
	13:31

[8]E. g., Boussett, *Kyrios Christos,* 42; Vielhauer, "Jesus und der Menschensohn," 170; Conzelmann, *Outline of Theology,* 131–37.

[9]E.g., Higgins, *Son of Man,* 1, 123–26.

[10]E.g., Tödt, *Son of Man,* 224–31, 293–96; Hahn, *Titles,* 28–34; Fuller, *Foundations,* 143–51.

[11]E.g., Vermes, *Jesus the Jew,* 185–86; Casey, *Son of Man,* 234–38; Hare, *Son of Man Tradition,* 257–82.

[12]E.g., Cullmann, *Christology,* 155–60; Moule, *Origin of Christology,* 11–22; Jonge, *Christology in Context,* 171–72.

[13]We see other examples of this in Matt 13:41; 16:27–28; 19:28; 25:31; and perhaps John 5:27.

[14]See also John 9:35–36; 12:34.

[15]See also Matt 11:19 and parallel; Luke 19:10.

[16]John 3:14; 8:28; 12:34.

[17]This seems to be presupposed by Bultmann (*Theology of the New Testament* 1.29–30), but he does not develop the point. Taylor explicitly adopts this position, but in a rather different sense than I do here (*Names of Jesus*, 32–35).

[18]Vermes ("The Use of *bar nash*"; *Jesus the Jew*, 163–68, 188–91), Casey (*Son of Man*, 224–40), Lindars (*Jesus Son of Man*, 17–28), and Hare (*Son of Man Tradition*, 246–56) argue in different ways that it was. Fitzmyer ("The NT Title 'Son of Man'") is dubious.

[19]See also Luke 12:8; Matt 19:28.

[20]On this see Callan, "Ps 110:1 and the Origin."

[21]Cf. also Acts 7:56.

[22]See the surveys of this title in Cullmann, *Christology*, 195–237; Hahn, *Titles*, 68–135; Vermes, *Jesus the Jew*, 103–28; Marshall, *Origins*, 97–110; Fitzmyer, "The Semitic Background of the NT *Kyrios*-Title"; "The NT *Kyrios* and *Maranatha*."

[23]E.g., Mark 7:28/Matt 15:27.

[24]E.g., Mark 11:3/Matt 21:3/Luke 19:31.

[25]See Luke 2:11.

[26]See also Acts 2:33–36 and *Barn.* 12.10–11.

[27]Cf. Heb 9:28.

[28]We find a similar interpretation of Ps 110:1 in 1 Cor 15:25; Rom 8:34 and Polycarp, *Phil.* 2.1. Here however, Jesus is seen as active during the interval between his resurrection and second coming. We will discuss this development below.

[29]On this see Glasson, *Second Advent*, 151–213. Other examples of the application to Jesus of Old Testament passages which speak about the coming of the lord may be seen in 1 Thess 4:16, which alludes to Mic 1:3, and 1 Thess 5:2–3, which alludes to Isa 13:6–8.

[30]On this see Fitzmyer, "The Semitic Background of the NT *Kyrios*-Title"; "The NT *Kyrios* and *Maranatha.*"

[31]Cf. also Rev 22:20.

[32]See surveys of this title in Cullmann, *Christology,* 270–305; Hahn, *Titles,* 279–346; Fuller, *Foundations,* 31–33; Vermes, *Jesus the Jew,* 192–222; Hengel, *Son of God;* Marshall, *Origins,* 111–25; Dunn, *Christology,* 12–64.

[33]E.g., Mark 13:32/Matt 24:36; Mark 14:36/Matt 26:39/Luke 22:42. This is especially common in the gospels of Matthew and John.

[34]Cf. Gal 4:6; Rom 8:15. M. R. D'Angelo has recently argued that *abba* in the New Testament does not necessari-

ly derive from Jesus' use of this word for God ("*Abba* and 'Father,'" 614–16).

[35]E.g., Mark 11:25; Matt 5:16, 45; 6:1, etc.

[36]E.g., John 1:18.

[37]On this see Fitzmyer, "*Abba*."

[38]Vermes, *Jesus the Jew*, 197–99; Hahn, *Titles*, 281–84; Hengel, *Son of God*, 63–64; Moule, *Origin of Christology*, 27–29; Jonge, *Christology in Context*, 167–69.

[39]Cf. John 1:49.

[40]Cf. also Mark 1:1; John 11:27; 20:31.

[41]Cf. Acts 3:18–21.

V. Jesus' Death As Atonement

[1]On this see Hengel, *The Atonement*; Williams, *Jesus' Death as Saving Event*.

[2]Hultgren (*Christ and His Benefits*, 11–23) argues that a focus on the future redemptive role of Jesus presupposes the redemptive significance of his death and resurrection.

[3]Cf. Rom 3:23–26; 1 Cor 5:7.

[4]Cf. 4 Macc 6:28–29; 17:21–22. On this see Lohse, *Märtyrer und Gottesknecht*; Williams, *Jesus' Death As Saving Event*, especially pp. 165–202; Seeley, *Noble Death*, 83–141.

[5]Hultgren sees the ultimate origin of this idea in Jesus'

disciples' experience of the risen Jesus and the presence of the Holy Spirit after Jesus' crucifixion (*Christ and His Benefits*, 25–39).

[6]On this see Hooker, *Jesus and the Servant*, 25–61; Cullmann, *Christology*, 51–82; Fuller, *Foundations*, 43–46; Leivestad, *Jesus*, 68–72.

[7]Jeremias, *"pais theou"*; Cullmann, *Christology*, 51; Hengel, *Atonement*, 72–75.

[8]Hooker, *Jesus and the Servant*, 154–63; Fuller, *Foundations*, 45–46; Williams, *Jesus' Death as Saving Event*, 203–29.

[9]Isa 42:1–4; 49:1–6; 50:4–9; and 52:13–53:12.

[10]Jonge, *Christology in Context*, 179–81.

[11]Fuller, *Foundations*, 44–45.

[12]On this see Cullmann, *Christology*, 13–50; Hahn, *Titles*, 352–406; Fuller, *Foundations*, 46–49, 50–53; Vermes, *Jesus the Jew*, 86–102; Leivestad, *Jesus*, 63–68.

[13]Other references to the death of prophets are found in Matt 23:29–36/Luke 11:47–51; Matt 23:37–39/Luke 13:34–35 and Acts 7:52.

[14]Fuller, *Foundations*, 127–29; Rowland, *Christian Origins*, 175–78.

[15]On this see Horsley, "'Like One of the Prophets.'"

[16]On this see Meeks, *The Prophet-King*. One link between

prophet and king is that both were anointed. Prophets are said to be anointed in 1 Kgs 19:16; Ps 105:15; and Isa 61:1. In 1QM 11.7–8; CD 2.12; 5.21–6.1; and 11QMelch 18 we find references to anointed ones who seem to be prophets, though they are not explicitly called prophets. Thus the word 'anointed' itself, used as a title for the eschatological king, could also be seen as applying to the eschatological prophet. Cf. Matt 26:68 where Jesus is mocked, "Prophesy to us, you Christ!"

As we have already noted (see Chapter III, n 1), Berger argues that the basic meaning of calling Jesus 'Christ' was to designate Jesus as the expected eschatological prophet (see also "Zum traditionsgeschichtliche Hintergrund"). Even if the argument is unconvincing, it shows the many points of contact between the expectation of the eschatological prophet and other strands of Jewish thought that were used to interpret Jesus.

[17]Cf. also Mark 8:28 and parallels.

[18]Matt 11:13–14; 17:10–13; Luke 1:17.

[19]See Dahl, "The Atonement: An Adequate Reward for the Akedah?" *Jesus the Christ*, 137–51.

[20]On this see Cullmann, *Christology*, 83–107.

[21]Heb 5:6; 7:17, 21.

[22]Cf. Heb 7:24–25.

[23]CD 12.23 and 14.19 speak of a single Christ of Aaron and Israel. This may reflect a later development in the thinking of the Essenes. See Dahl, "Eschatology and History in the Light of the Qumran Texts," *Jesus the Christ*, 49–64.

The eschatological priest can be called the Christ (= Anointed) of Aaron because the priests of Israel were anointed (cf. Exod 28:41; 29:7). Even more clearly than in the case of the eschatological prophet, the word 'anointed' itself, used as a title for the eschatological king, could also be seen as applying to the eschatological priest.

[24]See *T. Levi* 18; *T. Simeon* 7.

VI. The Belief That Jesus Now Reigns in Heaven

[1]On this see Fitzmyer, "The Languages of Palestine in the First Century A.D."

[2]This process may have already begun among Palestinian Christians. The Hellenists, first mentioned in Acts 6:1, may have been Greek-speaking Jews who had settled in Jerusalem. The translation of the Christian gospel which occurred spontaneously among them may have given rise to theological differences from other Christians which led to their persecution. They may have been responsible for the Christian mission to Damascus. Acts specifically says that they were responsible for the spread of the Christian message outside Palestine (11:19). On this see Hengel, "Between Jesus and Paul," *Between Jesus and Paul,* 1–29, especially pp. 26–29.

[3]E.g., *Ag.* 51.

[4]E.g., *Ab.* 121.

[5]Have the Corinthians (and in a different way, the Thessalonians) heard a preaching so focused on the present lordship of Jesus that they see no need for a future resurrection? This would explain how they could affirm

Jesus' resurrection as a presupposition of his present reign, but deny their own. Cf. 1 Corinthians 15.

[6]Moule (*Origin of Christology*, 43–44) makes a similar suggestion.

[7]Cf. also Rom 10:9 and 1 Cor 12:3.

[8]Moule (*Origin of Christology*, 35–43) argues that the estimate of Jesus implied by calling him 'lord' in early, Palestinian, contexts is not essentially different from the estimate implied by calling him 'lord' in a Gentile environment.

[9]Cf. also 1 Pet 3:22; Polycarp, *Phil.* 2.1.

[10]On this see Moule, *Origin of Christology*, 47–96; Jonge, *Christology in Context*, 112–23; etc.

[11]Cf. 1 Cor 15:21–22.

[12]These two stages are collapsed into one, and Christians are said to have already risen with Jesus in Col 2:12–13; 2:20–3:1; Eph 2:5–6. However, even in these passages the full significance of rising with Christ will only appear in the future (cf. Col 3:3–4; Eph 2:7).

[13]Cf. 1 Thess 4:16; 1 Cor 15:23. In 1 Cor 15:51–53 Paul explains that even those who are alive at the second coming, and so have no need of resurrection, must undergo a transformation in order to inherit the kingdom of God (cf. v 50).

[14]Cf. 1 Cor 10:16–17.

[15]Cf. also Gal 3:27–28 and Col 3:11.

[16]Cf. Acts 22:5–8; 26:11–15.

VII. Belief in the Preexistence and Incarnation of Jesus

[1]Moule (*Origin of Christology*, 138–40) makes a similar suggestion.

[2]Cf. also 1 Cor 10:4.

[3]Gal 4:4; Rom 8:3; John 3:16.

[4]Cf. also Col 1:15–16.

[5]On this see Fuller, *Foundations*, 72–75; Dunn, *Christology*, 163–212.

[6]The translation is that of Charles, *Apocrypha and Pseudepigrapha* 2.213.

[7]Fuller, *Foundations*, 72–75; Dunn, *Christology*, 168–76.

[8]Hamerton-Kelly argues unconvincingly that in designating himself Son of man, Jesus implied his preexistence (*Pre-existence*, 100–102).

[9]See Luke 11:49.

[10]On wisdom Christology in Matthew see Suggs, *Wisdom, Christology and Law*; Dunn, *Christology*, 197–206. H. M. Humphrey has recently argued that the gospel of Mark presents Jesus as Son of God in the sense that he is a righteous man into whom the Wisdom of God has passed

and thus through whom Wisdom makes her appeal to the human race (*"He Is Risen!"* especially pp. 58–59).

[11]Dunn, *Christology,* 187–94.

[12]Cf. also 1 Cor 8:6. Those who see the passage as presenting the preexistence of Jesus include Craddock, *Pre-existence,* 94–98; Hamerton-Kelly, *Pre-existence,* 168–77; Jonge, *Christology in Context,* 189–99.

[13]On this see Jervell, *Imago Dei.*

[14]On this see Cullmann, *Christology,* 249–69; Fuller, *Foundations,* 75–76; Dunn, *Christology,* 213–50.

[15]Murphy-O'Connor, "Christological Anthropology"; Dunn, *Christology,* 114–21. For the opposite view see Craddock, *Pre-existence,* 106–112; Hamerton-Kelly, *Pre-existence,* 156–68.

[16]Dunn, *Christology,* 121–23. For the opposite view see Craddock, *Pre-existence,* 99–106; Hamerton-Kelly, *Pre-existence,* 150–51.

[17]Dunn, *Christology,* 186–87.

[18]Cf. also Heb 1:6; 7:3.

[19]John 3:13; cf. 6:62.

[20]John 3:19; 12:46.

[21]John 3:31; 8:23.

[22]John 6:38, 41, 50–51.

[23]John 8:42; 13:3; 16:27–28, 30; 17:8; cf. 18:37.

[24]John 3:17, 34; 4:34; 5:23–24, 30, 36–38; 6:29, 38–39, 44, 57; 7:16, 18, 28–29, 33; 8:16, 18, 26, 29, 42; 9:4; 10:36; 11:42; 12:44–45, 49; 13:16, 20; 14:24; 15:21; 16:5; 17:3, 8, 18, 21, 23, 25; 20:21.

[25]John 1:18; 5:37; 6:46; cf. 1 John 4:12.

[26]John 3:11, 32; 18:37.

[27]John 3:34; 8:47; 12:49–50; 17:8.

[28]John 5:19–20.

[29]E.g., John 5:18; 6:41–42; 8:48–59; 10:31–39.

[30]John 3:16, 36; 5:24; 6:40, 47; 11:25–26; 20:31; cf. also 1:12; 3:18; 7:38–39; 8:24; 12:36, 46.

[31]E.g., John 12:23–24; 13:1, 31; 16:28; 17:1–5.

[32]John 3:14 –15; 8:28; 12:32–34.

VIII. Conclusion

[1]On the resurrection see Fuller, *Formation of the Resurrection Narratives;* Perkins, *Resurrection;* O'Collins, *Jesus Risen.*

[2]For example, Marxsen, *Resurrection of Jesus;* Schillebeeckx, *Jesus,* 380–92.

[3]For a parallel, but very different, attempt to use study of scripture to establish a hierarchy of truths, see Meier, "The Brothers and Sisters of Jesus."

BIBLIOGRAPHY

Hultgren, A. J., *New Testament Christology: A Critical Assessment and Annotated Bibliography* (Bibliographies and Indexes in Religious Studies, 12; New York/Westport, CT/London: Greenwood, 1988).

Sources

Charles, R. H., ed., *The Apocrypha and Pseudepigrapha of the Old Testament in English* vol. 2 *Pseudepigrapha* (Oxford: Clarendon, 1913).

Charlesworth, J. H., ed., *The Old Testament Pseudepigrapha* vol. 2 (Garden City, NY: Doubleday, 1985).

Lohse, E., ed., *Die Texte aus Qumran. Hebräisch und deutsch mit masoretisher Punktation, Übersetzung, Einführung und Anmerkungen* (München: Kösel, 1964)

Vermes, G., *The Dead Sea Scrolls in English* (Baltimore: Penguin, 1968).

123

General

Berger, K., "Zum traditionsgeschichtlichen Hintergrund christologischer Hoheitstitel," *NTS* 17 (1970–71) 391–425.

Betz, O., *What Do We Know About Jesus?* trans. by M. Kohl (Philadelphia: Westminster, 1968).

Boussett, W., *Kyrios Christos: A History of the Belief in Christ from the Beginnings of Christianity to Irenaeus* trans. by J. E. Steely (Nashville: Abingdon, 1970).

Brown, R. E., "Who Do Men Say That I Am?—A Survey of Modern Scholarship on Gospel Christology," *Biblical Reflections on Crises Facing the Church* (New York: Paulist, 1975) 20–37.

Bultmann, R., *Theology of the New Testament* 2 vols. trans. by K. Grobel (New York: Scribner, 1951, 1955).

Casey, P. M., *From Jewish Prophet to Gentile God: The Origins and Development of New Testament Christology* (Louisville: Westminster/John Knox, 1991).

Conzelmann, H., *An Outline of the Theology of the New Testament* trans. by J. Bowden (New York & Evanston: Harper & Row, 1969).

Cullmann, O., *The Christology of the New Testament* trans. by S. C. Guthrie and C. A. M. Hall (NTL; Philadelphia: Westminster, 1959).

Dahl, N. A., *Jesus the Christ: The Historical Origins of Christological Doctrine* (Minneapolis: Fortress, 1991).

Dunn, J. D. G., *Christology in the Making: A New Testament Inquiry into the Origins of the Doctrine of the Incarnation* (Philadelphia: Westminster, 1980).

Fitzmyer, J. A., *Scripture and Christology: A Statement of the Biblical Commission with a Commentary* (New York: Paulist, 1986).

Fredriksen, P., *From Jesus to Christ: The Origins of the New Testament Images of Jesus* (New Haven & London: Yale University, 1988).

Fuller, R. H., *The Foundations of New Testament Christology* (New York: Scribner, 1965).

Goppelt, L., *Theology of the New Testament* 2 vols. trans. by J. E. Alsup (Grand Rapids, MI: Eerdmans, 1981, 1982).

Hahn, F., *The Titles of Jesus in Christology: Their History in Early Christianity* trans. by H. Knight and G. Ogg (London: Lutterworth, 1969).

Harvey, A. E., *Jesus and the Constraints of History* (Philadelphia: Westminster, 1982).

Hengel, M., *Between Jesus and Paul: Studies in the Earliest History of Christianity* trans. by J. Bowden (Philadelphia: Fortress, 1983).

Hultgren, A. J., *Christ and His Benefits: Christology and Redemption in the New Testament* (Philadelphia: Fortress, 1987).

Jonge, M. de, *Christology in Context: The Earliest Christian Response to Jesus* (Philadelphia: Westminster, 1988).

_____, *Jesus, the Servant-Messiah* (New Haven & London: Yale University, 1991).

Jossa, G., *Dal Messia al Christo: Le origini della cristologia* (Studi biblici 88; Brescia: Paideia, 1989).

Keck, L. E., "Toward the Renewal of New Testament Christology," *NTS* 32 (1986) 362–77.

Kramer, W., *Christ, Lord, Son of God* trans. by B. Hardy (SBT 50; Naperville, IL: Allenson, 1966).

Leivestad, R., *Jesus in His Own Perspective: An Examination of His Sayings, Actions, and Eschatological Titles* trans. by D. E. Aune (Minneapolis: Augsburg, 1987).

Marshall, I. H., *The Origins of New Testament Christology: Updated Edition* (Downers Grove, IL: Intervarsity, 1990).

Marxsen, W., *The Beginnings of Christology: A Study in its Problems* trans. by P. J. Achtemeier (FBBS 22; Philadelphia: Fortress, 1969).

Moule, C. F. D., *The Origin of Christology* (Cambridge: Cambridge University Press, 1977).

Pokorný, P., *The Genesis of Christology: Foundations for a Theology of the New Testament* trans. by M. Lefébure (Edinburgh: T & T Clark, 1987).

Rowland, C., *Christian Origins: From Messianic Movement to Christian Religion* (Minneapolis: Augsburg, 1985).

Sanders, E. P., *Jesus and Judaism* (Philadelphia: Fortress, 1985).

Semeia 30 (1985) *Christology and Exegesis: New Approaches.*

Taylor, V., *The Names of Jesus* (London: Macmillan, 1959).

Vermes, G., *Jesus the Jew: A Historian's Reading of the Gospels* (Philadelphia: Fortress, 1973).

Vielhauer, P., "Ein Weg zur neutestamentlichen Christologie? Prüfung der Thesen Ferdinand Hahns," *EvT* 25 (1965) 24–72.

Christ/Messiah/Anointed

Berger, K., "Die königlichen Messiastraditionen des Neuen Testaments," *NTS* 20 (1973–74) 1–44.

_____, "Zum Problem der Messianität Jesu," *ZTK* 71 (1974) 1–30.

Charlesworth, J.H. *et al.*, eds., *The Messiah: Developments in Earliest Judaism and Christianity* (Minneapolis: Fortress, 1992).

Grundmann, W. *et al.*, *"chriō ktl.,"* *TDNT* 9.493–580.

Horsley, R. A., "Popular Messianic Movements Around the Time of Jesus," *CBQ* 46 (1984) 471–95.

Jonge, M. de, "The Earliest Christian Use of *Christos*," *NTS* 32 (1986) 321–43.

_____, "The Use of the Word 'Anointed' in the Time of Jesus," *NovT* 8 (1966) 132–48.

Scholem, G., "Sabbatianism and Mystical Heresy," *Major Trends in Jewish Mysticism* (Jerusalem: Schocken, 1941) 287–324.

Van Unnik, W. C., "Jesus the Christ," *Sparsa Collecta: The Collected Essays of W. C. Van Unnik* vol. 2 (NovT Sup 30; Leiden: Brill, 1980) 248–68.

Fulfillment of Scripture

Dodd, C. H., *According to the Scriptures: The Substructure of New Testament Theology* (London: Collins, 1953).

Gourgues, M., *A la droite de Dieu: Resurrection de Jesus et actualisation du Ps 110:1 dans le Nouveau Testament* (EBib; Paris: Gabalda, 1978).

Hay, D. M., *Glory at the Right Hand* (SBLMS 18; Nashville: Abingdon, 1973).

Hengel, M., "Psalm 110 und die Erhöhung des Auferstandenen zur Rechten Gottes," *Anfänge der Christologie: Festschrift für Ferdinand Hahn zum 65. Geburtstag* ed. by C. Breytenbach & H. Paulsen (Göttingen: Vandenhoeck und Ruprecht, 1991) 43–73.

Juel, D., *Messianic Exegesis: Christological Interpretation of the Old Testament in Early Christianity* (Philadelphia: Fortress, 1988).

Lindars, B., *New Testament Apologetic: The Doctrinal*

Significance of Old Testament Quotations (London: SCM; Philadelphia: Westminster, 1961).

Luke-Acts

Callan T., "The Background of the Apostolic Decree (Acts 15:20, 29; 21:25)," *CBQ* 55 (1993) 284-97.

Dahl, N. A., "The Purpose of Luke-Acts," *Jesus in the Memory of the Early Church* (Minneapolis: Augsburg, 1976) 87–98.

Esler, P. F., *Community and Gospel in Luke-Acts: The Social and Political Motivations of Lucan Theology* (SNTSMS 57; Cambridge: Cambridge University, 1987).

Fitzmyer, J. A., *The Gospel According to Luke I–IX* (AB 28; Garden City, NY: Doubleday, 1981).

Jervell, J., *Luke and the People of God: A New Look at Luke-Acts* (Minneapolis: Augsburg, 1972).

The Expectation That Jesus Will Come Again

Callan, T., "Ps 110:1 and the Origin of the Expectation That Jesus Will Come Again," *CBQ* 44 (1982) 622–36.

Glasson, T. F., *The Second Advent* (London: Epworth, 1945).

Robinson, J. A. T., *Jesus and His Coming* (Philadelphia: Westminster, 1979).

Son of Man

Casey, P. M., *Son of Man: The Interpretation and Influence of Daniel 7* (London: SPCK, 1979).

Fitzmyer, J. A., "The New Testament Title 'Son of Man' Philologically Considered," *A Wandering Aramean: Collected Aramaic Essays* (SBLMS 25; Chico, CA: Scholars, 1979) 143–60.

Hare, D. R. A., *The Son of Man Tradition* (Philadelphia: Fortress, 1990).

Higgins, A. J. B., *The Son of Man in the Teaching of Jesus* (SNTSMS 39; Cambridge: Cambridge University Press, 1980).

Lindars, B., *Jesus Son of Man: A Fresh Examination of the Son of Man Sayings in the Gospels in the Light of Recent Research* (Grand Rapids: Eerdmans, 1983).

Perrin, N., "The Apocalyptic Son of Man Sayings," *Rediscovering the Teaching of Jesus* (New York: Harper and Row, 1967) 164–99.

Tödt, H. E., *The Son of Man in the Synoptic Tradition* trans. by D. M. Barton (NTL; Philadephia: Westminster, 1965).

Vermes, G., "The Use of *bar nash/bar nasha* in Jewish Aramaic," in M. Black, *An Aramaic Approach to the Gospels and Acts* (Oxford: Clarendon, 1967) 310–28.

Vielhauer, P., "Jesus und der Menschensohn: zur Diskussion mit Heinz Eduard Tödt und Eduard Schweizer," *ZTK* 60 (1963) 133–77.

Lord

Fitzmyer, J. A., "New Testament *Kyrios* and *Maranatha* and Their Aramaic Background," *To Advance the Gospel* (New York: Crossroad, 1981) 218 –35.

————, "The Semitic Background of the New Testament *Kyrios*–Title," *A Wandering Aramean*, 115–42.

Son of God

D'Angelo, M. R., "*Abba* and 'Father': Imperial Theology and the Jesus Traditions," *JBL* 111 (1992) 611–30.

Fitzmyer, J. A., "*Abba* and Jesus' Relation to God," *À Cause de L'Évangile: Études sur les Synoptiques et les Actes offertes au P. Jacques Dupont OSB à l'occasion de son 70 anniversaire* (LD 123; Paris: Cerf, 1985) 15–38.

Hengel, M. *The Son of God: The Origin of Christology and the History of Jewish-Hellenistic Religion* trans. by J. Bowden (Philadelphia: Fortress, 1976).

Loader, W. R. G., "The Apocalyptic Model of Sonship: Its Origin and Development in New Testament Tradition," *JBL* 97 (1978) 525–54.

Atonement

Hengel, M., *The Atonement: The Origins of the Doctrine in the New Testament* trans. by J. Bowden (Philadelphia: Fortress, 1981).

Lohse, E., *Märtyrer und Gottesknecht* (Göttingen: Vandenhoeck und Ruprecht, 1955).

Seeley, D., *The Noble Death: Graeco-Roman Martyrology and Paul's Concept of Salvation* (JSNTSup 28; Sheffield: JSOT Press, 1990).

Williams, S. K., *Jesus' Death as Saving Event: The Background and Origin of a Concept* (HDR 2; Missoula MT: Scholars, 1975).

Suffering Servant

Hooker, M. D., *Jesus and the Servant: The Influence of the Servant Concept of Deutero-Isaiah in the New Testament* (London: SPCK, 1959).

Jeremias, J., *"pais theou," TDNT* 5.677–717.

Prophet

Horsley, R. A., "'Like One of the Prophets of Old': Two Types of Popular Prophets at the Time of Jesus," *CBQ* 47 (1985) 435–63.

Meeks, W. A., *The Prophet-King: Moses Traditions and the Johannine Christology* (NovTSup 14; Leiden: Brill, 1967).

Influence of Hellenistic Culture

Fitzmyer, J. A., "The Languages of Palestine in the First Century A.D.," *A Wandering Aramean*, 29–56.

Preexistence of Jesus

Craddock, F. B., *The Pre-existence of Christ in the New Testament* (Nashville and New York: Abingdon, 1968).

Habermann, J., *Präexistenzaussagen im Neuen Testament* (Europäische Hochschulschriften: Reihe 23, Theologie 362; Frankfurt am Main/Bern/New York: Lang, 1990).

Hamerton-Kelly, R. G., *Pre-existence, Wisdom and the Son of Man: A Study of the Idea of Pre-existence in the New Testament* (SNTSMS 21; Cambridge: University Press, 1973).

Humphrey, H. M., *"He Is Risen!" A New Reading of Mark's Gospel* (New York/Mahwah, NJ: Paulist, 1992).

Jervell, J., *Imago Dei: Gen 1:26ff im Spätjudentum, in der Gnosis und in den paulinischen Briefen* (FRLANT 76; Göttingen: Vandenhoeck und Ruprecht, 1960).

Murphy-O'Connor, J., "Christological Anthropology in Phil II, 6–11," *RB* 83 (1976) 25–50.

Suggs, M. J., *Wisdom, Christology and Law in Matthew's Gospel* (Cambridge: Harvard University Press, 1970).

Von Lips, H., "Christus als Sophia? Weisheitliche Traditionen in der urchristlichen Christologie," *Anfänge der Christologie*, 75–95.

Resurrection

Fuller, R. H., *The Formation of the Resurrection Narratives* (London: SPCK, 1972).

Marxsen, W., *The Resurrection of Jesus of Nazareth* trans. by M. Kohl (Philadelphia: Fortress, 1970).

O'Collins, G., *Jesus Risen: An Historical, Fundamental and Systematic Examination of Christ's Resurrection* (New York/Mahwah: Paulist, 1987).

Perkins, P., *Resurrection: New Testament Witness and Contemporary Reflection* (Garden City, NY: Doubleday, 1984).

Schillebeeckx, E., *Jesus: An Experiment in Christology* trans. by H. Hoskins (New York: Seabury, 1979).

Scripture and Hierarchy of Truths

Meier, J. P., "The Brothers and Sisters of Jesus in Ecumenical Perspective," *CBQ* 54 (1992) 1–28.

INDEX OF REFERENCES